THE Answer IS LOVE

Stories of **Personal Triumph** from Heartbreak to *Finding Answers*

EMILIA BRUCKNER

www.emiliabruckner.com.au

First published in Australia 2022 by Emilia Bruckner

ISBN 978-0-6456715-0-6

Disclaimer

All the information, techniques, skills and concepts contained within this publication are of the nature of general comment only and are not in any way recommended as individual advice. The intent is to offer a variety of information to provide a wider range of choices now and in the future, recognising that we all have widely diverse circumstances and viewpoints. Should any reader choose to make use of the information herein, this is their decision, and the author and publisher/s do not assume any responsibilities whatsoever under any conditions or circumstances. The author does not take responsibility for the business, financial, personal or other success, results or fulfilment upon the readers' decision to use this information. It is recommended that the reader obtain their own independent advice.

Dedicated to...

My Babcia (Polish Grandma), who taught me how to appreciate the small things in life, for showering me with unconditional love and making me addicted to the pursuit of it.

My Mum, who taught me about respect, discipline and that I am always loved as I am.

My Dad, who has challenged me and loved me a lot. Thanks to those challenges I have become the strong woman I wished to be.

My sister Ania, for loving me continuously.

My sister Dorka, for showing me what love is, and how to be strong and invincible.

My Children Marria, Nadia, and Luciano, for being the angels who held me up when I have fallen, and for loving and challenging me to be the best version of myself.

My husband Gary, for coming into my life when I needed proof that love can conquer all, and for showing me every day that I am worthy of everything that I have always dreamt of.

Table of Contents

IF YOU WOULD ASK ME,
WHAT WOULD I PREFER:
NOT TO LOVE
OR TO LOVE WITHOUT
BEING LOVED IN RETURN,
I WOULD ANSWER:
WHAT IS BETTER,
BUNCHES OF BEAUTIFUL
ROSES WITH THORNS,
OR ITS ABSENCE.

Preface

This book is not about telling anyone how to live their life. It is not a manual on how to find love or fix relationships. Instead, it is a true story of how I have fixed my relationship with myself, and how I found love. Not just in a romantic sense, but deep, unconditional love.

The kind that heals and gives the strength to move mountains, but also makes us as vulnerable as a child, all at the same time. A love that knows no fear, no limits and does not apologise.

If you choose to take my advice, I am certain you will taste that love and heal in you, what you may see as not perfect yet.

My journey has taken me to places in my mind that I did not want to go, places that kept me captive and I was the only one who could break me free. It is a journey that I would now happily take because the treasures I found are worth it.

I have lost my best friend and a happy marriage, but I have gained myself and become my best friend. I found a new companion who gave me the marriage that I have always dreamt of.

My family had to restructure itself, and children had to learn how to survive the tsunami of parents' moods and fears. It taught them not to take anything for granted, strengthened their bond with each other and me, and gave them priceless jewels of wisdom, even if they were hard earned and unwanted at the time.

Losing my sister felt like a piece of me was ripped out, but in its place grew an appreciation for life, with roots so strong that nothing can pull it from my heart. That appreciation made my life so beautiful, and all the fears now seem like small rocks to jump over.

Thank you for taking the time to hear my story. My wish is that you might see yourself in me, and perhaps in my struggle, you might find what you are looking for in life.

There is no better gift to yourself than the gift of having all the answers to the biggest questions.

I made this my own Mount Everest, my quest for answers, and I did not stop climbing until I reached the top. My peak had the answers I needed, and the view from there was so much more than I ever expected. I only hope that the mountains that you chose to tackle will provide you with amazing experiences, and that you will find joy and love while climbing them.

I have put on paper what I have been keeping in my heart for many years. Almost ten long years, to be more precise. It seems so unreal that it has already been ten years.

Ten years of what? Ten years of everything.

A sadness that I did not know existed.

A loneliness which I was sure was going to kill me.

A continuous struggle with my mind to let me be and let me stop thinking. A wanting to silence my mind from bringing up the past which felt unbearable, both real and unreal at the same time, a past so brutal and unfair that I was ready to fight every dragon to undo that reality.

Ten years of getting to know the person who was living in my head, trying to make sense of what has happened and why.

Ten years of the extreme lows, that lying on the cold bathroom floor the whole night felt like the only answer to the heaviness of my heart – a heart so done with feeling that only the coldness of the floor was able to seize the attention from the pain inside it, transferring the discomfort to the physical body instead.

It was also ten years of the most beautiful moments of heartfelt gratitude that I have never known, and I feel lucky to experience them.

Ten years of a very close-up and personal look at myself: Lots of talking to myself, crying, and feeling sorry for myself. Arguing with myself, swearing at myself, forgiving myself. Not liking and hating myself, as well as enjoying my own company.

Breaking myself into pieces and putting them back together over and over.

Introduction

I chose to write this book because I wanted to remember the journey I have been on. I did not want to forget the painful moments and the heartfelt revelations that have come about because of those sad moments.

My wish is that no part of my journey that was meaningful should be forgotten in case I forget that from the deepest lows grow significant highs.

Every moment of perceived loss was a moment of gained appreciation; times of darkness and feeling lost became moments of biggest discovery and finding that beautiful light in the dark tunnel of my mind.

I wanted to remember that the pain was so deep not because I was weak, needy of someone's love, but because my love, loyalty and determination was so strong, and I was not going to give up on what was important to me.

I felt very low mentally and acted desperately because my love was strong and giving up on that love was not an option for me.

This book is a testimony to my strength and what it took to be faithful to my heart that made me choose love. Not love for someone who chose to love me, but to love when love seemed like the last thing my mind wanted to choose.

It is my heartfelt wish that you will find my words and experiences helpful in navigating your own struggles with love, relationships, and the meaning of life. I hope you find inspiration and strength to keep looking for your own answers.

If this book helps even one person to overcome their mental struggles, their fears about the future or to find ways to carry love and appreciation in their hearts instead of resentment and anger, then my dream of being of service to others will be achieved.

Overcoming challenges is only one part of having an amazing life. Creating the life we want to live is another.

I have created for myself the life I wanted to live. I could do that because I have not given up on myself and kept true to my soul calling to keep choosing love.

In this book, I have included details of my journey and how everyone can use their imagination and wishes from the heart to live the life they always wanted.

There are two important insights that the reader will take away after reading my story.

First is that their love, their heartbreak, their pain, and their battles were all part of the road that they wanted to take, even when at the time it seemed insane. Second, that they are magnificent as they are. There is nothing that they can do or not do that was, is, or will be ever a mistake.

We all are creators of our own destiny, and allowing ourselves to acknowledge that is all that is needed to create a life full of love and purpose so we can always feel connected to ourselves, as well as to the people and the world around us.

Part 1:
Love is a Choice

A Love that Made Me Forget Myself

As I was standing on the river's edge, looking out at the slowly flowing water, my eyes filled with tears.

It was such a beautiful time of the day, mid-morning, with picture-perfect weather, blue skies, little wind and sunshine. Such beauty around and such darkness inside.

Whatever I tried to do – visiting new places, looking at the surrounding beauty, trying to hold onto nice thoughts – nothing seemed to be working. The increasing pain of loneliness was only added to as couples walked past, hand in hand.

I saw big rocks near the path, thought I would look stupid sitting on one, but I wanted the distance from others, and the pain of walking along the path with the increasing sadness weighing heavy in my heart dismissed the thought quickly.

I found comfort sliding onto the smoothest rock nearby, and as soon as I sat down, I closed my eyes and a few seconds of peace emerged.

I did not want to cry again. That was all I did at home, mostly while hiding in my bedroom. So, as I clenched a dry leaf that I had picked up from the ground beside me, I started to daydream.

I have always believed in fairy tales. Not because I have watched them as a little girl – far from it. There were no Disney movies or stories when I was little and growing up in Communist Poland. I used to read and imagine a lot to take myself to places where I wanted to be and who I wanted to be with.

My imagination was my saving grace, my escape from the reality I did not want to acknowledge. For as long as I could remember, I used to create my reality in my imagination, and for the 18 years with the first love of my life, I experienced all my dreams coming true.

For me it was not just blind belief, it was my way of creating, living, and enjoying life. I wanted to create a scenario that my thoughts could grab onto and hold for a while to escape the excruciating pain of a broken heart.

I could hear the birds, the wind, and I could feel my broken body not wanting for anything else but some relief from the emptiness that was submerging me.

I started to imagine that while I was sitting there sad and broken, I felt someone's hand on my shoulder. No, I would not open my eyes – in heaven you do not need to see with your eyes. You see with your heart.

He sat beside me and, not saying a word, took my hand into his. I loved those hands, strong but soft, and he caressed my hand as a mother would a child that felt sad and lost.

The first time he did that was on the day of our marriage, fifteen years ago when Uncle Mario walked me into that little chapel on Hayman Island, and when I approached him; he took my hand and kept touching it softly.

No words were needed. He was there, he found me, he understood that we belonged together. He used to say that he was the luckiest man on Earth because he found someone who loved him, and he loved me back. It's amazing how beautiful it feels to be near someone we choose to love.

He proceeded to put his arm around my waist and brought me close to him. I could not say a word or do anything but let the tears flow down my face.

I knew those hands so well – those soft hands made for a gentle touch.

Is it their love that fills us up so much that there is no room for anything else, or is it our love for them that fills our hearts to the brim, to the point that we are short of breath from it? As much as I wanted to stay in that frame of mind for longer, I was not able to. Sadness, loneliness, despair and fear came flooding my mind and sinking my heart again. I could not escape to my imaginary places as I used to.

Whatever I did to try and forget the depths of grief I felt, my mind kept me there. I felt like I was on the bottom of the ocean, suffocating and close to drowning.

The dark veil of anxiety took over my mind again, and there was nothing I could do to escape its claws. Tears rolled in and I gathered all the strength I had to walk slowly to the car where I could hide.

If Words Could Kill

When things started getting intense at home, I was doing what I could to hold it all together.

Not being able to talk to my husband the way we used to, was the worst part. Since he started listening to the teachings of his new guru, he closed himself completely to me. It was supposed to be all about love and light, but very little love extended to me. There was not a day that past where he did not spend hours listening to recordings of the man he chose to hold as an authority in his life.

I could not understand what happened to my open and loving husband. If he was learning love, why were we not able to talk? Why had I been pushed aside and ignored like trash?

That fateful morning, I was upset that he was never home and he had stopped communicating with me. I was struggling mentally, and I had no one to talk to. My mum and sisters were far away; with my friends, I could only cry for a bit, but I was not able to ask for the help that I wanted. I needed support to make sense of what was happening to my marriage, but I was left to face it alone.

I asked him if we could take some time and go away somewhere. Just him and me. He looked at me with cold eyes and said, “I don’t want to be married anymore. It is over.” Then he walked away.

As the saying goes, “If words could kill,” I felt as if those words were the killer’s hit. He asked my niece, who was at our place at the time, to look after me. My life fell apart.

I ended up in the hospital for a few nights, as my mind and body were not able to cope with the reality of what was happening. My marriage and my family were what I lived for.

The life we had created for ourselves in almost twenty years was magical in many ways. It had its ups and downs, but there was not a day that we would not say that we loved each other, and we made love often. We built a successful business, overcame financial challenges and faced family issues together. We grew as people, partners and parents.

Some of the most significant times were between 2007 and 2010 when he was having anxiety and panic attacks because he suppressed his emotions about family and business issues. He became more present with me and the children, and we become closer. He let himself be vulnerable and open. We spent lots of time together, and life was great. I thought that I knew my husband, and I trusted him. I thought that he knew me and trusted me.

I loved him like I have never loved and I would have jumped in to the fire for him. Everything I ever did was with him in mind. He was the one I wanted to see happy. I said yes to many things he wanted, just to make him happy. The one thing that I said no to – his new beliefs, his worship of his new god – was to end our marriage.

Before, I would agree to go along with his decisions to keep the peace and make him happy. This time, I was voicing what bothered me and wanted to be heard. I was hoping to be considered, and while he was experiencing with his new faith, I hoped we could keep loving each other.

Gratitude has Given Me My Life Back

It's amazing how words can make you feel so beautiful inside as if you were falling in love. Something so sweet, exciting in different places and making you gasp for breath, all just from writing something.

The word that triggered that for me was *appreciation*. But... appreciation for myself.

Incredible.

It's a feeling that I was only able to recreate in my body, during moments when I made love. I was looking to name the *journey* that led me to finding it, and I choose to call it *Appreciation for Myself.*

All the battles that I fought with myself – the ones I thought I do not want to fight – were so worth it.

For that beautiful moment *now*.

I was thinking about how I could show it to others, how I got there and how others could experience it if they choose to, then my life and my dream would continue in them.

I was sitting in a coffee shop in Cairns writing those sentences in my diary. Five years had passed since I was put onto the journey of discovering myself.

My diaries have been my best friends since I was fourteen. I started writing on the Christmas Eve of 1981 while in my grandmother's home in a small village in Poland. It was winter, it was cold. There was no TV in her house. While the family was busy with each other, I felt like I could not talk to anyone about what was going on inside of me. So, my diary was my escape to pour my thoughts and feelings onto paper. His name was Krzysiek, and he was two years older than me, and according to that old diary, we were a "couple" for the last two years.

I was interested in boys for as long as I can remember. I wanted to be noticed, I wanted to feel like I mattered. I did not want to be in a relationship with them, I just wanted a confirmation of my existence somehow.

Looking back, I think it was because I felt like no one knew me from my family, like no one wanted to look at me and truly see me. I craved being noticed, craved being truly seen, craved for someone to take the time to listen and understand me.

Now, sitting in that lovely coffee shop where I was meeting with my friend, that appreciation made my soul soar. By chance, I had my diary with me, so I kept putting those words onto the pages. I felt so grateful and so much like a heavenly peace was in me and around me.

The reason for my appreciation came from reflection: three years before on a previous visit to Cairns, I was in so much despair in such a crisis, like the world was pushing me onto my knees and mental pain was my constant companion. That is why being there and feeling on top of the world felt so great.

As the saying goes, we cannot experience the highs unless we experience the lows. So much wisdom and truth in that.

We fight so hard to avoid anything that feels uncomfortable, that threatens our imagined way of living, but unless we get pushed to our knees, or even forced flat on the ground from the temporal heaviness that life dishes out, we can never know how amazing it feels to be out and standing tall, free of the fears that got us there in the first place.

There were other significant reasons for the flooding of those indescribable emotions. I was waiting to see Irene. She and her husband were the first Australians I met in Italy. While living in Italy and dating the man who would become my first husband, I met Irene and her husband, who were his close friends. We met during the winter, and we had a crazy time enjoying sledding down the slops in northern Italy. After arriving in Australia, they became my friends as well, and they have been part of my life for almost twenty years.

Cairns was where we lived before we got married and where I had many happy memories from my marriage and as a family of five. After the separation many painful memories were created here as well, that is why it felt so good to be on the other side of it.

I was in Cairns, as it was from here that I and my second husband would take off to fly to Europe for our honeymoon. It's amazing how life can change in just a few years. That is, if we decide what kind of change we would like to see in our lives. We then have a choice to do what it takes to achieve what we want, and I believe that I have learned the secret recipe to having everything that we desire.

The most important part of it is to keep using the recipe and keeping this goal in mind. Writing this book is a part of wanting to pass on that knowledge. We can get old while trying to work out what life is about or grow old knowing.

I finished writing those words about how amazing it felt to be grateful just as Irene arrived. I let her read that one page, and she said that she would like me to write a book so others can learn what I have learned through my experience. I said that I will do just that.

It started slowly, but her confidence in me gave me the wings to fly back into my memories and find those nuggets of gold that I want to pass on to everyone and anyone who wants it.

Paradise is Here on Earth

The sun was shining through the sliding glass doors. I loved my glass doors opening onto the patio, welcoming the sun in through the day.

Sitting at my dining table, I could see not only all the flowers I had planted in the big pots to enjoy all the colours and shapes, but also the trees around the garden, the blue skies soaring above and my favourite birds singing from the branches nearby. It was my new paradise, just as I had dreamt it, but even more beautiful than I saw in my imagination.

It is proof that you can rise from the ashes of a broken mind, broken heart and everything else that made up your safe haven before you were plunged into the darkness, where fear was ever-present and death seemed so close.

As I looked across the living room and gazed at Gary, my husband of six years, I felt that the love and joy that filled my heart was so intense that it made me short of breath, and tears would start to well.

This is it. I have arrived at my safe harbour; I have climbed my own Mount Everest that I set out to climb.

When I began the journey almost ten years ago, lonely, crushed by the weight of total disconnection from my then-husband, not knowing where to turn and mostly not seeing the road ahead, I did not know where I was going to end up.

At the time, I could not have imagined that I would be able to love so much again. But there I was, being loved and I loved again with all my heart. Something that I had thought was not possible to have again. The love and dedication I had for my first husband were so intense, that when he said that he did not love me anymore, I collapsed into the darkness of depression and grief.

It took me three years to crawl back from the darkest place I have ever been to. The darkness clouded my mind to the point of considering cutting my life short.

These thoughts haunted me, even despite having been blessed with three beautiful children, a close and loving family, a large group of dedicated friends and financial stability.

The hardest thing was that I could not understand what has happened to the person that I used to be. That mature, confident, successful woman who trusted her intuition, who knew how to act in any situation. I had fought many battles before, crossed countries, learned languages, worked in managerial positions and was never scared of any challenges.

But this time I could not see a way out and accepted being defeated by continuous anxiety. Every battle

I fought in my head as I tried to conquer the fears and desperation, I lost. I was scared like a child who knows only how to cry when scared, without any other way to get out of a frightening situation.

I had never been a stranger to the harshness of life, but such sadness, anger, betrayal and loneliness I had never faced before. I trusted my then-husband, and he chose to turn my life upside down.

Every Crisis is a Blessing

I turned to writing in the hope of healing my mind and heart. Was it the pleasure or the pain that I wanted to put onto paper so I could make peace with it and leave it where it belongs... in the past?

No matter how beautiful or ugly our past is, it is gone forever. And it stays there, in the past. The beautiful memories stay as those beautiful moments; the ones that we did not enjoy as much, become lessons. I believed in that.

I loved loving others and learning how to appreciate everything that I have encountered along my journey. Those many moments that become the lessons were still present in my memory with a tint of sadness. I knew in my logical mind that every crisis came with a blessing, but my fragile heart was still weeping, and every time I thought of those times, tears would come extremely easy if I allowed myself to go there.

So, I wanted to do that, to gather all those moments that I still saw as painful and relive them. Relive them with every single detail of pain that made me gasp for air and took away the strength to continue.

I spent thousands of hours of balancing my mind and found gratitude for those moments. Literally thousands, and it has saved my life.

It saved me from wanting to end it and the misery of seeing it repeatedly in my mind. I wanted to love instead of hate but did not know how, and it was excruciating. It also saved me from the continuous anxiety that crippled me every second of every day.

I faced those memories with all that I had, and it worked. It worked wonders.

After starting to see glimpses of my old self, I promised to never allow myself to get to that place of extreme anxiety again. I could not do it again. I had made it to the other side of the bridge. I did not drown in the ocean of my tears or from the wounds in my heart.

I understood how someone can die from a broken heart, and how painful it is to live with one. It is a mental and physical experience, like having knives pushed into your chest all day long. It's unbelievable how our mind, when convinced of loss and with repeated thoughts, can create such a painful physical experience.

I saw the power of the mind. Not moving mountains and creating anything it can imagine, but the other side, the one that takes you downhill. I saw how destructive it can be for the body, and how quickly it can rob it of strength, adding pains we did not know existed.

The Person I Did Not Want to Become

I did cross that bridge, one small step at a time.

One of the important encounters on my journey towards recovery was a lady who was nearly 90 years old. Her story made me promise to change what I was doing and, most importantly, what I was thinking.

My son was playing a soccer game. He has always been a great soccer player since he was five years old. His ability to play and his enthusiasm on the field were so great that I have always enjoyed watching him play. I would even make comments that watching him play and score was as good as sex. I never said it to him, of course – he was too young to hear it then. But at that time, I was not able to enjoy it at all. Even worse, having people around me that I knew and not being able to hold a conversation without thinking that I would burst into tears was painful. All I wanted to do was hide away from everyone.

There was a sports club across the road, and I went there with the excuse of getting a coffee, but I just wanted to sit in the corner alone and wait till the game was over.

I sat in a coffee shop area where there were not many people. Shortly after I had taken a seat, an old lady with grey locks walked towards my table and asked if she could join me. I agreed. She said that she lived in an assisted living facility and was dropped off to pass some time. I was not interested in talking, but I smiled back politely. Then she asked me how I was. I thought, what the heck, I don't know her, I may as well be honest and tell her how I felt.

The story of how my husband walked out of the marriage and how heartbroken and depressed I was poured out of me. I told her how I found it almost impossible to keep going and how I did not know what to do.

I was hoping for some words of wisdom that she might have, but she did not offer any. Instead, she agreed that what happened to me is awful, and that she understands because her marriage did not last as well.

She proceeded to tell me how her husband cheated on her with his secretary, left the marriage and took most of the money. He died of cancer almost twenty years ago, but she could still remember all the wrongs he did.

I was sitting there with my eyes wide open in disbelief that this lovely lady had only critical things to say about her husband, who was not even alive anymore. She still had lot of anger towards him and saw his actions as punishable and wrong.

She did not offer any words of wisdom, but instead, she gave me something much more valuable. I realised who I did *not* want to become. I did not want to spend my life being a victim of someone's else actions. I did not want to live with memories that brought back the anger and sadness. I did not want what happened to me to become my legacy of a broken person, wearing those painful moments as badges of honour from the battles I survived.

I did not know if I would be able to switch off my sadness and find a balm to heal the deep wounds in my heart. That day I was still so deep in the well of my despair, but she made me even more desperate to keep praying and looking for a cure, to look for something that would turn the anger off. Something that would allow me to love my husband again, regardless of what he has or has not done.

Finding Gratitude

It was summertime, early evening, two years on from the time when the sky collapsed and brought me to my knees. I was sitting on the rocks surrounding a big palm in my garden.

I loved that spot. I looked at that majestic palm every day, admiring the beautiful white flowers planted around it by my mum. It had been my favourite view from my window for the last sixteen years. During the many hours of every day, I would look at that exact spot through my kitchen window, whether it was to find relief from the never-ending housework or to watch my children play in the garden from the day they were born.

While sitting there, for the first time in two years, I stopped feeling anxious for a few minutes. My mind was a peace, and I felt normal again. It did not last long, but long enough to notice how good it felt.

What changed was how I chose to see what has happened in my life. Instead of looking at those painful events and seeing the abandonment, rejection, betrayal and hurt, I chose to see that those painful events over the last two years had other sides to them. The side that I was oblivious to before, the one that had brought in many blessings. I found gratitude. Practicing gratitude helped me combat the mental fog and the weigh of pain that filled my heart when it got broken. I have tried everything I could think of to help me with the pain that filled my heart, and I could not understand how it was possible to love someone so much and feel so much pain at the same time. Every fibre in me was trying not to be angry at him, and I wanted to shout loud to the world how big my love for him was. But the pain of a broken heart was all I could feel. Enormous, relentless pain, even when I would hug my beautiful children or think about others who I knew and who loved me very much. I tried to sleep – it was my escape for months. Sleeping pills became my best friends. I tried every doctor that was able to shed some light on my state and ease the mental burden. I tried praying – lots of praying, church groups and church counsellors, psychologists, psychiatrists.

I tried alternative therapies and all kinds of calming drinks and pills. I tried writing, to pour my pain onto paper and hope to leave it there.

I tried telling others in the hope of easing the burden. I thought I tried it all.

But when the days turned into weeks, weeks into months and months into more than two years, and I was still in pain, I knew that what I was doing was not working.

Seeing so many others walking around with the same regrets and painful memories many years after the events made me promise to myself to find a way to conquer that pain and to love again.

Love Heals

The love I had for him did not disappear. It turned into a decision to love him, because I loved myself more when I decided to keep loving him.

The discovery that loving someone does not mean that we must have them love us back with their presence and their actions was the breaking point on my journey to healing. I have learned that we can choose to love someone deeply, regardless of that person's actions towards us.

That is true love, love with no conditions placed upon others. That love, if we are genuine, heals. That love we can feel, as it takes up all the space of our heart, not leaving any space for doubt or worry.

I started having glimpses of it. Bit by bit, I was able to focus on just appreciating and loving him instead of what I wanted from him. I felt glimpses of normality, moments of being present with myself and with life around me. It was working.

Someone called that kind of love gratitude, a true appreciation for someone exactly as they are, and that kind of love started the healing process. I knew that there was no turning back to complaining, criticising, blaming, resenting or wanting. Not that I was free from those emotions, far from it. I just knew which road I had chosen to move forward.

Gratitude, unconditional love and acceptance of him as he was. Acceptance of the past, acceptance of the present and acceptance of what the future will bring. That kind of gratitude that I have learned to have for him and for others has transformed my life forever.

It was the person who I thought has hurt me so much who has given me the biggest gift.

An unconditional feeling of appreciating others as they are and not wanting to change anything in them, not wanting to rewrite any parts of our past with them or fearing for our future with them.

I used to think that I had lost the most precious things in my life: the man that I loved so much, the marriage, the family, the stability of having a place I called home for my children, the foundation my children had to feel safe and loved.

When I felt abounded, lonely and lost, I felt like if the Earth had opened beneath me and there was nothing to grab on to in order to save myself from falling into the deep hole of desperation. I wanted to die, and those thoughts were breaking my heart; to continue living feeling so empty, so shaky, so useless, so broken and in so much pain was too much sometimes. Finding gratitude gave me the ray of sunshine I was waiting for to grab on to and cling to life. It gave me my first glimpse of hope for recovery.

Love for My Dad

The journey of my life is what I wanted to relive. As much of it as I could bring back in my memory. I believe that our lives can be as beautiful as our imagination can create them. That is how we can create an amazing life for ourselves. It was not just a belief for me, but a known fact.

As a little girl, when I would go to bed I would close my eyes and create in my imagination whatever I would love to experience.

I did not want for material things. I did love beautiful things and felt jealous seeing my friends having new jeans or pretty clothes, but what I was imagining was a handsome boy next to me. I wanted to be noticed, liked and have someone who would care about me.

Imagining a very handsome boy cuddling, kissing and giving me all their attention was my daily routine. Later, I discovered that it was probably the need to be seen and heard – which I translated into being loved – that I was looking for.

By now I know why I was looking for attention, acceptance, and a close bond with a man. I believed it was because I have never experienced it with my dad.

I adored my dad. He was kind, funny, very tall and handsome, with amazing blue eyes and cheeky smiles. People loved him. He was the heart of every party, as well as a very hard-working person.

He only had one hand – the left one. He lost his right hand in an accident on his parent's farm while operating machinery. He was sixteen years old when it happened.

Later, he went on to do an apprenticeship as a welder and learned to write beautifully with his left hand. I was always amazed how he was able to do so much just with one hand.

He welded pretty things for our home, made a sled for winter, sewed his clothes when they needed repairing and was great with horses. He also worked full time. Unfortunately, I did not have too many of those good memories with him.

He liked alcohol. And often he would come home from work very drunk. Those days would be the times when my world would turn into a nightmare, a nightmare I had no chance to escape.

I hated him for that, I hated my life and could not understand why I was being punished by God to have to live through it. I felt angry, embarrassed and hopeless. There was not much I could do when I was little, but I knew that I was not ok with that.

Later I understood that my need for recognition from men came from that lack of having my dad's attention as I would have loved. I have often thought that if only he would know how much I loved him. If he had chosen to notice that love and feel it, I was convinced that he would be happy and would not need alcohol and his drinking friends.

Meeting Grief for the First Time

We become the product of what we have experienced and how we have perceived it at the time. And, if no one will correct that perception for us, we often end up living life thinking that someone has hurt us and did not love us as we wanted to be loved.

At the time of my childhood and teenage years, that was my way of seeing myself and my life. I felt as though something was missing in me, as I was not enough to be noticed or worthy of receiving my dad's love. I have never stopped loving my dad, but I did want him to die, wishing that my life would be free of his abuse and fear of what the day will bring.

I have contemplated jumping off the balcony of my apartment – not that I wanted to die, but I remembered having those thoughts. I could not understand life and why I was experiencing one that often seemed liked a punishment.

I survived my teenage years, walked into adulthood with courage and hope, and moved abroad. One year into my Italian adventure, I was to face the loss of my father.

The last time that I saw him, he was very proud of me that I worked overseas, knew foreign languages and was earning good money. He had been on a disability pension for a while already, but he never stopped working. At that time he was employed as a handy man at a mechanical shop.

One winter evening, I got a phone call that he had passed away. His aorta burst while he was on his way to work early in the morning. He was found under the tree that he had probably used to support his fall. Just like that, he went to work and never came back.

While I was overseas, I used to visit every six months. This time I had not visited for a year. After finishing the season in the hotel where I met my future husband, I agreed to do a babysitting job for the family of jewellers that I worked for the year before. They wanted me to help during the busy time before Christmas.

My dad passed away on the 7th of December, and it was one year on from when I saw him for the last time. I organised a trip by train to Poland. It was very strange to see this handsome, still young man (he was only 50) laying there without life in him. He still had his very thick hair.

I visited the morgue and kissed his cold forehead, then I travelled with him in the van, to the place one hour drive away, to the town which was central to the area where he and mum met, and where they came from.

I was angry with God at that time for taking him away so soon and so tragically, with no one next to him.

Interestingly, two months before I met the man that I fell in love with and who I was to marry. They say that when God takes someone away, he replaces them with someone new. For me, it was a man who gave me what I wanted and became my everything for the next nineteen years. He was tall, like my dad; he was handsome, like my dad; he loved people, like my dad; he loved to laugh, like my dad; and he worked hard, like my dad.

Waiting for the "Aha"! Moment

Life is an amazing gift, full of an array of experiences, people, places and emotions.

We seem to swing like a pendant from likes to hate, wants to wants nots, having to not having. Then, from time to time, we stop and try to make sense of our decisions, the actions of others and those experiences.

Some will find answers that make sense to them and they will be at peace with the daily journey, while some keep searching and questioning themselves, others and God.

For as long as I could remember, I questioned everything about myself, the actions of others around me and I have had many conversations with God.

By the time I was 44, I was married to someone I loved and felt loved by very much, had three children that I felt immensely blessed with, had the house of my dreams, a busy social life and good financial stability, but the questions about life were ever-present.

It felt like there was a hole inside of me, and whatever filled it would be there only temporarily.

That "aha!" moment that gurus talk about was something that I was trying to find. I was not sure what was missing in my life, but something very important was absent because I did not love nor accepted myself as I was. And consequently, I was not accepting of others as they were.

During that time, I considered myself to be a kind, appreciating, very caring person. I was always there for others, and I was proud of it.

Life was good to me, and lots of people would love to have what I was living, so when thoughts and questions would overwhelm me, I would turn to my diaries to scribble it down on the paper and leave it there.

I was trying to find answers to why I would not feel happy while I had everything I wanted. At the time, I did not know that to have those answers I had to take the journey of discovering who I was.

Living Life to the Fullest

After surviving my childhood and learning that my life was up to me, I have had a great run.

I have never waited for anyone to give me what I wanted, instead I went and organised it for myself. I worked hard and partied hard. I finished high school with a trade as an expert on books. Took two months holidays to travel with my best friend through Poland with a backpack and a tent. After returning to Krakow I found work with Government agency.

All those years were filled with countless examples of me trying my skills and building my confidence in many areas. There was so much that I did and was proud of myself for having a go and not having many fears.

I knew hard labour from working at my grandparent's farm, looking after animals or collecting hay, so I would be allowed to play with friends till the early hours of the mornings during weekends and school holidays.

I worked on school camps as a cleaner and kitchen hand during school holidays.

I was a young scout, then a leader who helped to set up new scout groups.

I joined a dance school and entered dancing competitions.

I acted in a play for children to earn money.

I was one of the main marketeers to organise a theatre performance for a new coming actors, which was a success.

For few years I was part of a church group that looked after young and older people with different disabilities and I was voted in as the treasurer. With that group I went on different camping trips, took part in many parties, travelled through Europe and even claimed mountains, pushing wheelchairs and assisting blind people up the mountains. I took part in a pilgrimage to the Black Madonna, assisting people in wheelchairs, walking for days and sleeping in hay barns.

During one of those adventures, while travelling through Europe, I was proposed to by a handsome English man in the front of Eiffel Tower. On another, in Munich, I was almost raped, and my life was threatened. I visited Russia and sold Polish jeans in the markets and bought Russian gold.

I have climbed peaks and slept in chalets in the wilderness, watched the moon reflected in a lake buried deep in the mountains, sat by the fire listening to beautiful music played with guitars and sung many songs that touched my heart.

I took part in a night-long slide down the hills in Italy under a full moon. I have sung with singers from all over the world, staying in the camp with worshipers of all religions of the world, in a little town called Taizé, in France.

I danced at many venues till the early morning, from country discos to the best venues in Poland and Italy. I visited most European countries and had lunch with mafia bosses while in Palermo. I crossed English Canal on a Cruise and hitchhiked from Poland to Italy.

I Learned Russian, English, Italian and German, and worked in managerial positions using three of them. I worked for Polish Government as an Inspector, travelled the country, slept in many hotels, cooperated with police, and appeared in courts. I worked as a fruit picker, a nanny and a restaurant manager in Italy.

I met the Consul of Morocco while dating a Moroccan boyfriend. I have met many people, was in love many times and had my heart broken often. I loved my life, and I have never expected others to look after me, but I loved looking after others.

By the time I met the man who become my first husband, I knew myself. I knew of life's challenges as well as its beauty. I fell head over heels in love with him. He was charming and handsome. I left everything that I loved in Europe and came to Australia to be with him. It was not easy to find myself on the other side of the world and to rely on him for almost everything. The saying that love can move mountains and conquer everything was put into practice as I have started my new life.

How I Forgot Who I Was

Looking back at what I have done and achieved on the way, it is almost unreal to accept that this person who was not scared of anything could feel so low and be so hopeless.

That girl, who would run in the middle of winter to the police station to try to help her mum, asking for her father to be arrested. That girl who would go to school after not sleeping the night because my dad would come home late at night and be laud and abusive. That girl who would fight her dad physically when she was sixteen. That girl who was told that she would be killed if she would not have sex. That girl was scared and helpless because the one who she trusted the most, told her that he does not care about her anymore.

That is the reason I wanted to write my story. It is the collision of what we think we are and what we could handle, and what could happen when we let our minds take the wrong turn. The difference between what we put into our minds and, consequently, what we will feed our hearts can be the difference between life and death.

I did not know it at the time, but I created a fantasy in my head that my happiness depended on how someone will treat me. I have also taken second place in my own life. I did what I have learned as a young child when I took it upon myself to protect my mum but forgot about how I felt or what I needed. I wanted to be the strong one who can help and protect others from harm.

My life demonstrated how I always wanted to be there for others, to help and support, but I have not learned how to ask for support, and most importantly, I have not learned that I was worthy of that help, care and support.

When I would ask, I would be afraid that I may take someone's time and they would have to put some effort into doing something for me. Somehow, I did not feel important enough to feel at ease with that.

During my first marriage, I would ask my husband if he could give me five or ten minutes of his time because I wanted to talk about something or needed help. I would try to let him know that I will not take much of his precious time. I was honouring his existence, and I saw his time as precious to him, but I was disregarding my own importance.

It was not his fault that I felt like I was not important – I put myself in that place by the ways I spoke and acted. I felt undeserving of much, and as a result, I was getting back crumbs of his attention.

I would suppress my disappointment and sadness when I was told that what I needed was not important to him. I would run to my diaries and pour my pain onto paper, telling those pages how unfairly I was treated and was trying to make sense to myself. Why was I not sticking up for myself? Why was I not asking to be treated with importance? Why was I not celebrated as someone that he professed to love dearly?

Those questions were constant in my head, and the pages about my pain and sadness at the time could make a book on its own. What I did not know then but do know now, is that none of that what his fault.

My reasoning followed established lines of criticising others if I was not spoken to nicely or if I was turned away without being helped or if I was shown no respect in front of others.

I grew up wanting the nice, not the mean; the support, not the challenge; the respect not the disappointment. Just like most of us did.

The turning point during my depression was accepting that our lives demonstrate what is going on inside of us. The thoughts that we keep thinking, the beliefs we hold as so-called our truth. Beliefs are nothing more than the thoughts that we keep thinking and accept as the truth. Those thoughts, if repeated often enough, rule our daily lives. How we feel, what kind of emotions float our hearts, is the consequence of those thoughts.

If we get told that something is good or bad, we then experience our outside world through those filters. We learn to want for the good and run away and reject the bad. That way of thinking was a cause of my depressive thoughts and fluctuating anxiety levels.

What I have learned since and tested over the years is that there is no definite line between so-called good and evil.

It is our perception of what we think supports or goes against our current values. We are only following our instincts that direct our thinking towards what we perceive will give us more perceived benefits over the perceived drawbacks.

The word *perceived* is the key to unlocking this mystery of how we see the outside world. Outside events are not just one-sided. Where one person will call an event as good or normal, someone else may call it bad or disturbing.

I kept thinking about that a lot when I was wrestling with my mind, trying to switch off the anxiety button, and a good example of what reflected my situation at the time is the following.

In some cases during a separation, one of the partners may decide to end the marriage, and the other may go into depression, feeling as though life is ending for them. Equally, the same person may realise that it could be a time for celebration, feeling free and excited about the future.

The same event has two different ways of looking at it: it all depends on what we want from life, what our top values are and how we are choosing to perceive what is going on around us.

Part Summary – Key Points

1. Gratitude turns our lives around from seeing events as positives and negatives to neutral events.

   Appreciating everyone heals us.

   Being open to and choosing love brings more love in.

2. Other's anger has nothing to do with us.

   Our happiness does not depend on how others treat us. Choose to love others regardless of what they do.

3. Our perceptions shape our lives.

   Nothing is one-sided.

   Choosing to see both sides bring balance to the mind.

Part 2:
The Love Story

My Italian Adventure

It was my second year in Italy. The year was 1994, and I was 27 years old. I ended up in Italy by chance.

The year before, a handsome policeman that I met during my travels while working for the government wanted to take me for an all-expenses-paid holiday to Greece. I took time off from work but changed my mind about going with him. I was worried that he would take it as my commitment to him, and I was not ready to commit. To date, yes, but not getting serious about having a life partner yet.

Instead, I and a girlfriend decided to hitchhike to France via Italy. We were in France the year before, in beautiful Taizé, where people from all over the world visit to pray and have fun together.

A year before, she met a handsome French man while we were together during the international youth meeting in Prague. I knew a handsome Tyrolian man from Northern Italy, whom I met in Krakow. She had an invite to visit Marseille in France, and I had one for Northern Italy. We had a plan to travel through Germany and Austria and stop in Italy for a week, then to Marseille, then to Taizé in France.

My Italian friend opened his home for us. He and I started a little romance, and we were asked if we want to earn some money, working for his friend who owned vineyards. We agreed. Work was hard, picking up grapes but the money was great.

I liked him and loved what I was earning so decided to stay in Italy longer. I got a leave from work, and my friend went back to continue her studies. The romance fizzled out, but we remain great friends today. From working in fields picking grapes and apples, I got a job as a nanny and housekeeper for a family of doctors in Terlano. After working for them for a year, and six months for a family of jewellers in Bolzano, I was ready for a change.

At that time, I had a great friend in Monika, a beautiful Polish girl that I met through my Austrian friends. We became close, and I used to spend nights at her place – a small room next to the hotel where she worked.

I slept on the floor in my sleeping bag, as there was only one small bed in her tiny room. I had rented a room in the town but liked spending time with her. I preferred to sleep on the floor in her room, instead of in the apartment of an old, strange man, where I had a room.

We became like sisters.

Looking for Love

While working for the jewellers, I met the brother of my boss. He liked me and we started seeing each other, keeping it a secret from my boss.

Paul was a music teacher and musician. He would take me to many concerts where we would enjoy classical music. The interesting thing was that my previous boyfriend in Italy was also a musician.

While visiting one of the churches in Terlano, I heard someone playing the organ beautifully. It was late afternoon, and I went to the small village church to thank God because my employers decided to organise a working visa for me. The church was empty. Just me and the beautiful music. I decided to go up and thank the person who played for me while I was praying. I was expecting to see a priest or an older organ player.

To my surprise, a young, handsome man with a head of curls and child-like blue eyes turned around, hearing my steps on the wooden staircase. He greeted me with a big smile, and although I could not speak German at the time, I was lucky because he spoke English very well.

Werner offered me a lift home and invited me to visit the church again. I did and ended up dating him for six months. He even visited Poland with me for Christmas.

But back to Paul. He kept telling me that I was too smart to work as a nanny and organised for me and Monika to meet the owner of a 5-star hotel in a village where he conducted a choir. I had never worked in any restaurant but lied that I did, and I got the job.

The hotel was up a mountain in a picturesque village overlooking a huge mountain range. It was called Romantic Hotel Turm. It is still there, as magnificent as when my love story started. Later, when I look back and consider how my story unfolded like a fairy tale, even hotel had a romantic name.

While working there with Monika, we had the best time. Work was hard, we worked for breakfast, lunch and dinner. We were sharing a room and loving life.

One day, we were told that a chef from Australia was arriving. We were super excited as we both spoke English but were using only German at work and learning Italian in our spare time. I finished the lunch shift and was going to my room. The staff rooms were in a building next to the hotel, and as I entered the hallway, I saw a tall, young man. He turned around and I said first in English, “You must be the new chef?” With a smile, he said, “yes.” He was very handsome and very friendly. We chatted and organised to go for a drink at the local pub after the evening shift.

Monika joined us, and we had a great time till very late that night. I liked him straight away but was afraid that he would be more interested in Monika because she was much prettier, but he chose me, and my fairy tale started then. It had its ups and downs while we were living in Italy, but it had so many highs.

My Fairy Tale Wedding

Before I met him, I have never given another man a second chance. If we had disagreements or someone was not 100 % in, I have always moved on.

With him, I did not. There were times when I probably should have run, but I was faithful to my heart. And my heart kept saying that he was the one – even the painful moments were not enough to scare me away.

I have never regretted listening to my heart. And choosing him was one of the best decisions of my life. I followed him to Australia and fell in love with his family, which substituted for the close family I left behind in Europe.

Finding myself in a new country again was a challenge I was open to embracing. There was so much happening and so fast, that it felt like a dream, not only because the places I was getting to know were taking my breath away, but because he turned out to be everything that I always wanted and more.

Our wedding on Hayman Island was one of those moments when I had to keep reminding myself that I was not dreaming. He looked so handsome, and I was his princess. The chapel was on the top of the mountain on one of the most beautiful and picturesque islands in the world, and the view was breath-taking. The day was sunny, with few clouds floating around, a small breeze, local birds, palms and local flowers setting the occasion like something from a fairy tale. It was my fairy tale, and I was more than ready to experience all that I had imagined for myself.

Those are the moments in life when everything stops, and we soak up every second and know that there is nowhere else we would rather be. For me, it was one of those moments.

Despite not having anyone from my family or friends with me, I felt that I had my best friend by my side, and my heart was full of love for him and the whole world.

Uncle Mario, who I chose to stand in as my father, and who I loved and respected as such, walked me down the aisle. I looked at my future-husband smiling at me. He looked very handsome, happy, and relaxed. His brother was by his side. His parents smiled at me, and I could feel the love and acceptance they chose to have for me as I was about the enter their family. For that love, I was then and forever after very grateful. They became the family I so desperately wanted and cherished as I became a mother and needed to recreate what I left behind in Poland. The family was a big part of my life and having such a big new one was helping fill in that part of my heart.

The Beginning of the End

Fast-forward fifteen years and there we were, a family of five, still madly in love with each other, holding hands wherever we went, making love often, never missing a day to tell each other that we cared and loved each other.

There were tough times to get through as well, mostly around running multiple hospitality venues and his family issues, but through it all, we had each other. Then, that faithful day I heard, "I don't want to be married anymore. It is over."

A few months before, there were tensions about the direction of his new spiritual beliefs. Those were too extreme for me and were putting everything I knew and believed about life upside down.

I was asked to follow the directions of his new guru, who was putting fear in his followers' hearts and asking them to follow his directions to obtain salvation through his teaching. Those teachings involved avoiding music other than that made by his followers, avoiding certain food and buying pictures that he designed that were blessed by him and had protecting powers from people with "negative" energy.

I met this man as well and saw straight away that he was selling fear and somehow convinced his followers that his visions gave him the powers to predict the future and tell others what to avoid in life to be safer in the afterlife. People in need of hope or spiritual guidance gathered around him, but I could not. Being told that I can't read anything else but his writing, or my husband asking my son to pray to a picture of the Mona Lisa (he was the reincarnation of Leonardo Da Vinci, among other reincarnations), was too much for me.

I trust people and the world around me and being told that if I drink milk "I don't know love", and that places or people could be "negative" was very distressing, and my mental health was declining.

But through it all, he was beside me, said "I love you" every day, and like so many other storms before, I was sure that our friendship, dedication and that true love that we often spoke about was going to get us to the other side.

I was wrong. Very wrong.

What came next what like living in a scary movie. Someone I thought I knew and who I trusted became disconnected from me.

Anxiety and Depression

There were so many moments, days, weeks and months when I thought that my heart would not be able to cope with the sadness and fear, and it would burst, ending my suffering. There were so many moments of anger and rage that I thought that there must be someone or something who could make it all right for me again.

There were countless phone calls to my still husband to come back, or at least communicate with me. There were many visits to services that I hoped would help, from police, community and government services to psychologists and psychiatrists. They were all there to hear my story, but no one had an answer on how to turn my head off and to heal my heart.

I was not able to make sense of what was happening. I was not interested in being right and making him wrong. I wanted answers to what was going on in my head and my heart. I could not believe how love could make someone want to die.

When the anxiety and depression forced me to my knees, I would cry all the time, unable to switch my mind off from the sad thoughts of not being loved by my husband and losing the family I knew so well. Thoughts about ending it started appearing. I would drive somewhere, and the thought would pop in that if I hit the oncoming car then my pain would end. There were times when I would hold the antidepressants or sleeping pills in my hand and think if I could do it to my children. Thinking about them saved me.

The youngest, my son, being only nice then, was trying to help me as much as he knew how. He would come to my bedroom where I was spending most of the time and check if I needed anything. He would bring in a glass of water or try to make some food.

My oldest girl would try to talk me out of obsessing about the love I had for my husband and tell me that from her point of view, he did not deserve me and my love. Her younger sister would sit with me and express how sad she was that the family was falling apart.

They did what they could to support me and care for me. It was my role to be there for them, but for almost three years the roles were reversed. It was thanks to their support, their maturity and mostly their love for me that I pulled through and wanted to be whole again.

After trying the well-established road of seeing the professionals in the field of psychology and psychiatry and not having any results apart from confirmation that I was a victim of someone's actions, I decided to do the work on my mind myself.

I decided to go back to studying what life is about, how our mind works, what the rules responsible for our emotions are and how our relationships with others and the world around us works.

The Wisdom that has Turned My Life Around

Back in 2007, my husband and I attended seminars run by Dr John Demartini, the founder of the Demartini Institute in Texas. The reason that we were drawn to those was that at the time we were having trouble dealing with one of our business partners.

His dishonesty and financial losses that followed were causing my husband to be extremely stressed and anxious. A friend gave us his book, *The Breakthrough Experience*, and inspired by its wisdom, we took trips to big cities to attend numerous seminars to find answers.

We both loved what we have learned about life and the rules that applied to all areas of life. The worries my husband had about his business partner have shifted and were replaced with appreciation for all the experiences. He was also able to find answers concerning his likes and dislikes about his parents. He started to be more in touch with his emotions, and was at ease with expressing them, embarking on the journey of seeing how everything that we experience from others serves us and how being grateful for those opens our hearts, lifts all the burdens and allows us to have peace of mind and a happy life.

We have both learned that taking responsibility for our actions instead of blaming others was the only way to feel empowered and to avoid depressive states of mind. Those teachings gave us all the answers that we were looking for and made us very close at that time; they become my saving grace when I choose to stop listening to those who were enforcing the victimhood mentality on me.

In 2014 I signed myself on to some courses again. It was one of the best decisions in my life: investing in myself to empower myself.

Our freedom is the best thing we can have in life. Freedom is the wisdom to know that everything that is happening to us, everything that we feel, depends on us and we are the only ones responsible.

Finding that out gave me freedom, and I know now that the key to keeping it is to take responsibility for myself and every action. Only then was I able to be strong, to be independent, to be free.

The Price of Freedom is Taking Responsibility

Everyone can be free. The price to pay is to take full responsibility for where we were or are in life. To take full responsibility for myself was to not blame anyone for how I felt or what I was experiencing.

If we do not want to take responsibility, we cannot have freedom. The two walk together. When we choose not to take responsibility, we accept one of the forms of slavery. In choosing to blame others or our out-of-control circumstances, or following others' ideas about our lives, we lose our freedom.

I chose to take my life into my hands – in the end, it is *my* life. I chose to follow my heart, which did not want to judge, blame or to make others responsible for where I was or how I felt. I chose not to follow others' ideas about what I should do or feel. By following others, we lose ourselves, and we lose our freedom.

At the time of my crisis, my family and friends were offering lots of advice. They all wanted me to get better, they all cared, but somehow, I knew that the advice was not in agreement with my heart, with the directions that I wanted to take in life.

The first step was to work out how to stop feeling sorry for myself , the second was how to stop being angry at my husband for leaving me and for the actions that followed. The answers lay with learning to love others as they are, and what follows was loving myself as I am.

When I started having the taste of how it feels to love myself, I regained my freedom. From that place, and only from that place of loving myself unconditionally, I was able to offer that love to those around me. I was able to give love to others because I had plenty of it for myself, but not from the place where I would give because I expected something in return. It was no longer exchange for me. I gave without expecting anything in return, and knew that I was getting love in return, regardless of others' actions. It was the freedom I was searching for.

Love is not something we can limit. It is not something we can hold back. When we try to put limit on love and hold it in, it escapes; when we open the tap and let it flow, we have plenty of it to give away as we please. When we choose to give it freely, it becomes limitless for us and others.

So, I have searched and found all the answers to what was killing me from inside. I was withholding love by judging my husband, I was withholding love from myself. I was professing my love to him to try to convince him to come back, and I was telling everyone who would listen how much I loved him. But I was also closing the flow of love because I was doing it from a place of sadness, a place where I felt sorry for myself and where I was portraying him as a perpetrator and myself as a victim.

I understood that we cannot have love and judgment in our hearts at the same time – the judgment cancels the love. That is why we experience anxiety, because we move away from love and our soul is making us aware that we need to stop and do something about it.

I have learned the most important lessons about life and love. The truth is that if we love someone then we will not try to change them, because when we love, we love everything about them – the beauty and the beast in them, the hero and the villain, the perfections and the imperfections.

When we want to change something in others, it means only one thing: we only love some parts of them.

Love gives freedom.

The Power of the Written Word

I love reading and writing. Those two played a major part in my recovery and how my life unfolded. Before I went back to study with Dr John Demartini again, I would try to read anything and everything that would help to ease the pain of my depressive states.

I will be forever grateful to my mum for the gift of loving reading that I have inherited from her. She was born in 1943, during the Second World War. Times were very tough then. She told me stories of when she was small, that she only had candles in the evenings when she wanted to read.

One of the books that I had, and I always thought that it was more to teach about business than emotions, was *Think and Grow Rich* by Napoleon Hill. In one of the chapters, it says:

"Memories of love never pass. They linger, guide and influence long after the source of stimulation had faded... Every person, who has been moved by *genuine love* knows that it leaves enduring traces upon the human heart. The effect of love endures because love is spiritual. The man who cannot be stimulated to great heights of achievement by love is hopeless – he is dead, though he may seem to live.

Even the memories of love are sufficient to lift one to a higher place of creative effort. The major force of love may spend itself and pass away, like a fire which has burned itself out, but it leaves behind indelible marks as evidence that it has passed that way. Its departure often prepares the human heart for a still greater love."

Books like this one and many others have helped me to recover my sanity. The written word had the power in it to switch off my mind and calm my heart. Holding a book in my hands gave me more strength and courage than anything else ever did.

Written words are our thoughts or other's thoughts organised in sentences that imprint themselves into our minds. Many underestimate the power of the written word, but the written word was always very important to me.

Our every thought is a word that we have learned, and that word has a meaning for us. We say words, we think words that we organise in sentences. Our lives become a stream of words that we say, think, write, read. Words are important, very important, maybe the most important part of our lives. Words create our thoughts.

When we have a thought that is pleasing to our mind, like that we are hoping for something or making a choice to see blessings in our lives, that thought is very fragile, and the wind of other thoughts will usually try to push it away very swiftly. It can be hard to hold onto the positive thoughts somehow.

Yet, the negative ones come on like avalanches, one after the other, then we get snowed down by those and the outcome is a depressive state. To be able to hold onto the good thoughts, I took time to find a piece of paper, a diary, or anything I could write on. I would take time to write what I wish I could think.

When a negative thought would flood my mind, which often happened suddenly, while I was doing some chores at home, I would stop what I was doing, find my diary and write ten positives to the one negative that I was perceiving at the time. I say perceiving, because with time I came to understand that our perceptions will name something negative or positive, regarding what we value in life.

I would make time to stop, sit down and write. If it was an angry thought about my husband, I would find things that were positive about having him in my life, like having the gift of my children, the memories of fun times, the places we visited together, the opportunities I had because I met him.

Those thoughts put on paper will do the trick every time. I would be that much calmer and closer to being able to deal with life in a better way.

Born to Love

They say that we do not come to truly understand life until we reach our forties or fifties. It seems to be the time when we start asking important questions and find the answers, or continue living dissatisfied.

I had those questions at the age of twelve, when I started questioning God. I would look at myself in the mirror and ask, *Why is me – me? Why do I look the way I do? Where do my thoughts come from? Why was I born in this country, to these parents?*

Many of us have those questions come up and we settle for simple answers, such as only God knows. I wanted to know who God is, and why would he make me go through the experiences that felt like punishments. I had questions, and I was angry with God from an early age.

But while he kept testing me with those people that I did not understand, where I felt like I did not fit in; he has also given me lots of courage, and the most important one – a heart that wanted to love above anything else.

All my life I was searching for the one thing that I considered most important – to love and be loved. Aren't we all?

All religions tell us that love is the pinnacle of our existence, that love is that fleeting something we all want to strive towards. Love heals. Love creates. Love gives freedom. Love is never-ending. Love is everywhere. No one can escape the idea that we are meant to love and we want to be loved.

I was one of those crazy romantics who believed that love was all those things and more. I chased love when I was little and wanted to be noticed; I chased love when I was a young teenager, trying to always look good so I would attract attention; I chased love during high school, dancing my way into love every weekend.

But the love that I wanted was evading me somehow. I did date. I fell in love and I was told that I was loved. All those did not last more than a few months. I was the one breaking it up and others were breaking up with me. Anytime I came close to having someone committing to me, I would find reasons to end it. I needed the experience to get to know myself.

Looking back, I thought I was just lonely and that was why I was trying to find connections with men. Later, I decided to call it research on what love is. Like a scientist that is trying to invent the best product or improve the existing one, like someone who conducts experiments in their research.

I was a scientist looking to find what love means, what love makes us do and what love is meant to feel like. I wanted to go through all the pains and pleasures that love has to offer.

Love is a Balance of Support and Challenge

Life happens on the border between support and challenge.

That truth I learned from Dr John Demartini. Love is a perfect balance of support and challenge. There is no love where there is only support; there is no love where there is only challenge.

The moment we say that we only want to be supported by someone but never challenged, we deny the parts of them that are challenging for us. When we say that we are happy for them to just challenge us but refuse support, we reject that side of them.

Like yin and yang, plus and minus, black and white, day and night. They exist together, both are necessary and one cannot exist without the other.

Love happens on the border of these opposite actions, the support and the challenge. Those who are around us and love us will do both, they will support us when we need it and challenge us when we need to grow.

While challenged, it can be difficult to see the other side, the support that is present. While challenged, it is not easy to see the benefits to it at that moment. It took me some time to accept that the balancing force is always there, and once I did, it became so much easier to love and understand those around me.

Those times when I was perceiving being abandoned and hurt by my husband, the opposite force was at work simultaneously. While he moved away from me and chose to stop loving me, other people become closer to me and started loving me more. My family, friends and my children started focusing on me more, telling me often that they loved me.

At the time when we perceive something negative and stressful happening, we are usually blind to the other side, the one that is creating a balance to what we are perceiving is happening. Nature does not allow anything to occur without the perfect balance.

When I was trying to recover from my broken heart through the established channels of healing from those events, I was unknowingly putting my mind out of balance, and the result was anxiousness. My soul was trying to wake me up from being blind to the magnificence of life.

I was agreeing with my counsellors that someone had hurt me, so I was holding onto the idea that there was only a challenge present at those moments of my life that I perceived as painful. When I took every moment that I perceived as one-sided and only hurtful and looked for the balancing blessings; I was able to find them every time.

That was the Holy Grail I was searching for my whole life: the knowledge that every event has its opposite and equal balancing side was the answer to my questions about the fairness of life. Whenever I was rejected, someone was accepting me more. When I was being let down, someone was there to support me. In the moments when I was told that I was not loved anymore, more love was proclaimed by someone.

I healed my mind by doing the exercises to find enough blessings in every crisis until it was neither positive nor negative, but a neutral event.

Once my mind could see the logic of every event, my emotions were able to calm down, and anxiety and depression started to lift. The glimpses of feeling normal again made my determination to keep going unstoppable.

I had the answer to what love is, I had the answer to what life is about, and I had the tool to heal my wounded heart. That tool made it possible to ignite the fire in me again, to want to love without limits and to share it with others.

Part Summary: Key Points

1. Freedom is taking responsibility of our actions. Choosing love gives us freedom from anxiety.

2. Stress is often caused by a lopsided perception of a situation.

3. Everyone is a reflection of us.

   We have what we admire in others, just as we have what we despise in others.

   We are always perfect as we are, with nothing to be changed, just to be loved.

4. Life is a balance of support and challenge.

   All events are neutral, until our mind chooses to see only one side.

   Every positive event is equally negative; every negative event is equally positive.

Part 3:
Love has Saved Me

Surviving Depression and Picking Up the Pieces

One year passed since my life was flipped upside down.

My husband moved out, the family as I knew it was gone and I no longer knew the person that was living in my body. I was existing somehow, getting from one day to the other, but there was a fog in my head and a heavy weight in my heart. Neither of those was lifting, and I got used to waking up sad, crying and feeling down during the day, then going to bed with the hope that some miracle will occur and my life will go back to normal.

My husband would not communicate with me. Instead, he sent me a letter from his solicitor that arrived on the 22nd of October 2012, the day of our wedding anniversary. It would have been our 15th. I was cut off from our accounts and told not to enter our business. I begged him not to involve the solicitors due to the cost, and every time I said that I would sign what he wanted me to, it was met with silence, as was every other attempt to discuss the children or many other issues. I did not know how to cope, and because I was clinging to the hope that he would come back, I was truly stuck.

I asked his parents, brother and sister to stay with me and help me recover, to help the children, but there was no response. No one was interested. Instead, I was told to ask my family in Poland to come and take care of me.

My mum and two sisters lived in Poland. Both sisters had full-time work and were the only bread winners, so as much as they felt for me and wanted to help, they were not able to come. I kept begging my mum to come, but she was afraid of travelling alone. I was not getting better, and after many cries on the phone, my mum said yes to coming over.

When she arrived, I met her at the airport with the children, and she started crying while walking towards us. The reason was that he was not with us. My mum loved my husband very much and was as heartbroken as I was seeing that he was not a part of the family anymore.

Having my mum at home was great for the children. There was someone who would talk to them, hug them, cook for them. She was not able to grasp why I could not shake off my sadness and be normal again. She would get upset with me when I was not able to drive her to church, saying that I could not think straight and the effort that took was too much sometimes. I tried to tell her many times that I wish there was a switch in me that I could flip, to turn off the thoughts in my head. Anyone who deals with depression has that wish. For those on the outside is not easy to understand.

In January 2013 we took a trip up north as a family. My husband chose for all of us to travel, as we used to, and visit his family. The children were happy, my mum was happy, I was happy. But my expectations of some resolution and happy family times were dashed when he continued to be distant and disconnected from me. There were many humiliating situations when I would beg for attention or connection, and received none. One evening while there, I was so distraught that I put sleeping tablets under my pillow and cried my heart out and thought of ending it.

Living with Guilt Made Me a Victim

After we returned from the holiday up north, I had to face the reality that my husband was not going to come back, and I needed to somehow start picking myself up.

My hope that we had travelled together to his family, and that he might have missed having me around, was destroyed. The hope that my mum coming over would somehow help him to turn away from the group that had become his family, was also gone. He spent many weekends in Brisbane and on retreats with the followers of his new beliefs.

My struggle was not only emotional but financial as well. His cutting me off our business and accounts, and only putting money in my account when he would agree to it, was very stressful. There were times when I had no money for petrol to take the children to school, or I had to beg him to agree to some transfers to be able to take our son to his soccer tournaments. Our business was still operating as usual – he was running it as he always had – but the savings that used to be put in our account on weekly basis from the business had stopped. He did not allow me to enter the business or investigate the books for the business.

I went along with it, as having him angry at me was hurting me more than the financial struggles. For a long time I could not understand why I used to be so hurt when someone was angry with me. I would try to do everything in my power to resolve every situation, but when met with anger and rejection of communication, I would suffer and torture myself with thoughts that maybe I could have done things better...It was a way of thinking that got me nowhere. People get upset and angry with us, and that does not mean that we could have prevented it.

I did not know it at the time, but I realised that there was usually nothing or little that I could have done to somehow protect others from getting angry at me or to protect myself from their anger. I lived with guilt for many years. If I only acted differently, if I was calmer if I was more loving, if...

That way of thinking was pointless. Whatever we have done or not done it cannot be undone. We did our best. Not much else to it, and beating ourselves up that we are who we are is soul-destroying.

I had to realise that I could not have been more loving, more beautiful, sexier, more ambitious, more everything else, for him to decide to stay. It was never about who I was, it was about him wanting more from life. I could not have been more of something to keep him by my side.

I believe that he has made up his mind about leaving me some time before. During our separation, I was sending him letters apologising, agreeing to accept his new beliefs, as hard as that was, proclaiming my love to him over the phone, tempting him to make love to me. I tried everything that I could think of. The lovemaking part was the only one that I succeeded at, and we made love at odd times, till my trip to Poland in March 2013. I was convincing myself that we were making love, but he would say every time that it was only sex for him.

At that time, it did not matter to me that I was treated like that. I was like a person who was drowning, and he was the only one who could pull me out to safety.

From Fear to Hope

There is more strength in us than we think we have. In moments when we do not see a way out, there is an invisible veil of protection that exists inside of us. That invisible force knows that we want to live, it knows that we have forgotten that we are loved by everyone. It knows that all we want is to show others how much we care, how much we love and how much we want to turn our thoughts from sadness to joy. That force will do what it can to turn our attention to what we truly want to see, feel and love.

Hope is not just a thought; hope is the beginning of a manifestation of all those things we wish and hope for. Hope is a part of the substance of creation. Everything that has ever been created started as an idea, a thought. From there it progressed to hope that it would become part of our experience. From hope, there is a short distance to having that what we wished for.

Like fear, hope is a force that, if given enough focus and attention, will take over our lives. We create from the place of faith or fear. Whatever we give our attention, our faith or fear will grow and manifest itself as a part of our lives.

I have learned that lesson the hard way. My thoughts were consumed with fear that my husband does not love me and my marriage will end. There was no room in my head for anything else but all the negative thoughts about him not wanting me. Weeks and months of obsessive thoughts about how distraught I was and fearing him not being a part of my life have created exactly what I feared, and much more unpleasant situations than I could have anticipated.

Since then, I have learned to notice how certain thoughts will make me feel. When I focus too much on the heavy ones – the ones that drag me down and create a brain noise that is not easy to switch off – I do whatever it takes to turn them off.

My teacher and mentor Dr John Demartini says, “What we think about and thank about we bring about.”

He added the word thank to the sentence because if we are thinking about something that bothers us, we will get more of things we will not like. Being thankful for what life is giving us brings more of that which we can be grateful for. Thinking about that what we want and being thankful as if that was already part of our life brings it to us faster.

The more grateful we are, the more we get to be grateful for; the more we complain, the more we get to complain about. It sounds so simple, but not many will use that formula. We get so used to seeing what we do not like, overthinking it and talking about it, that it becomes our favourite past-time: focussing on that which is not wanted.

Unfortunately, most people design their lives that way and end up facing challenge after challenge because they focus and talk more about the problems instead of the good in their lives. I used to be one of those people. I used to worry about other's behaviour towards me, and other's behaviour towards others. I was trying to fix the world by thinking that if everyone did everything the nice way, my life and their life would be somehow better.

How naïve was I? Now I know that from those worries I was only making myself feel down, and that I was only attracting humbling situations to teach me to be grateful instead.

The Truth About Life and Love

Once I learned that truth about life, I looked back at the times when I used to judge other actions and where thinking like that got me.

I remembered a time when I was very upset about someone dear to me. Her husband had cheated on her and moved out. The whole night I could not think about anything else but how sad I was for her. The following morning, I woke up and I could not talk because my voice was gone. I could not understand what caused it. I got it back the next day. Now I know it was the universe sending me a very powerful message to try not to focus on something with such a force, and most importantly, to not focus on thinking that someone is wrong, bad or that someone is a victim of something.

My worries contributed to lots of health issues and have robbed me from having joy in my life. I would feel sick in my stomach a lot, and it was my body's way of trying to tell me that I could not stomach a situation or event. I could not stomach it because I was focusing on problems. Those are not problems that we see, those are actions that we apply our imbalanced perceptions to.

Life just is, but our values and perceptions shape how we see something. We judge something as good when it supports our values, and we judge something as wrong if it goes against our values.

In relationships, no one is faithful to us, everyone is faithful to their values. Our partners choose us because we represent what is fulfilling their values, and we apply the same rule while looking for a partner. As soon as some of those values are not being fulfilled, our nature makes us look towards other partners who may fulfil those values. The so-called "love" that we feel towards someone is our need for having in life that, which gives us a sense of security and fulfilment. That person that we say we love gives us what makes us feel special, chosen, appreciated, wanted and one of a kind. That someone takes time to be with us, to hear us, to compliment us, to take care of us. It makes us feel valuable and significant. It makes us feel like we belong, like our existence has value.

It took me almost 50 years to work it out. The love I felt for my first husband felt so real, so deep, so good and so overwhelming at times. I loved being in love, and I loved thinking that I was loved. His decision to stop loving me was devastating because it felt like I was losing something that was like a life force for me. I could not understand how someone could become so important to me that his decision to not be around me would trigger thoughts of suicide. How could love do that? How could love to cause us to want to end life? For all those questions I would have no answer for many months while suffering after my marriage breakdown.

Healing My Mind, Healing My Body

The truth that I discovered later was that life gave me those experiences because I have asked for them. I wanted to know what love truly is. I wanted to know how to love unconditionally. I wanted to be loved and not to have questions about how genuine it is. I wanted others to know how much I love them. I wanted to love so much that there was nothing else that was more important than that.

I could not have learned it any other way but to have experienced what the so-called love is. The attachment to the idea, the expectations, the wanting others to change for us. The non-existent feeling that we call love had to be investigated, and my definition of love had to be reshaped.

I was asking the big questions, and the universe was spitting up the answers. The more down and upset I would get, the worse I would feel. My soul was screaming for love. It was making me feel awful to stop doing what was not working and to start choosing love.

We cannot have judgment and love in our minds and hearts at the same time. I thought that my sadness was the result of a love lost and that it was the right thing to fight for that love. I was wrong. Choosing to blame, to be a victim, to judge other people's actions is far from love. When we choose that road – when we feel sorry for ourselves, for someone else or we are plain angry – we move far away from love.

Our minds and bodies do what they can to wake us up to ourselves and to stop doing it. When the brain noise gets too heavy, we need to stop and choose our thoughts more carefully, otherwise, we hurt, and we hurt badly.

Anxiousness is not a fun mindset to be in. When the mind will not be listened to and the destructive thoughts continue, our body will try to help us as well. The pain that it will create is a tool that our body uses to help us to wake up from the lies we have been feeding our brains. It is the body's last resource to try to bring our thinking back to balance. Pain is never an enemy, it is not a punishment from the above, it is our friend who is on our side.

When I was anxious, I would feel very sharp pains in my chest, so painful that I had to bend down and stop what I was doing. It was as though someone had stabbed me. The pains would be felt in different areas of my chest, but always not far from where my heart is. I knew that it was my mind cultivating the thoughts of a broken heart and the body would respond by stabbing me around my heart to make me stop.

I did not stop, but I did choose to monitor my thoughts, and how I was perceiving what was happening around me. Five years later, while my wounds were healing but the perception of being victimised was not fully cleared, I was diagnosed with rheumatoid arthritis.

It is a disease where our own body attacks its immune system. I was told that it is incurable and all I can do is slow the progression of it. How fitting. I was the one who kept attacking myself by feeding the thoughts that were firing into my body. I did it to myself. I did not stop when the pain went from just mental to physical. In some way, I kept asking for the physical pain, as I thought that it was easier to deal with.

Since then, I have healed my mind enough so that my body had a chance to be free of that disease. Incurable is always curable from within, and the body that creates the disease has the ability to heal it.

A few years after the diagnosis, I received the news that I did not have it anymore.

Depression is an Absence of Love

When my head was so full of thoughts that were making me cry, I would hit my head onto the tiled walls in my shower to try to silence my head. Many nights when I was not able to fall to sleep and wanted my head to stop thinking, I would lie down on the tiles in my bathroom, because then I would get cold and my body would start hurting after lying down on cold tiles, and my mind would have a rest.

When I was back to normal, one of my friends who was dealing with emotional and physical abuse said that she often preferred physical violence to name-calling because the words hurt more. It is harder to wipe out the words from our minds than it is to heal the physical wounds, it seems.

I know now that it is not the person who we choose to blame for hurting us that is doing the damage. It seems controversial that it is not their fault. Everyone will have their journey and understanding of how to see their experiences and what lessons to learn. Mine were powerful ones, and the outcome was to see those who we perceive as hurting us as our messengers of love.

My perceptions about life and about love were distorted. I was wanting for love – and as a result, life – to be just one-sided. Only supporting, agreeing with only my needs, keeping me in a safe place.

Love, like life, is a synthesis of opposites. We don't know what is good unless we know what felt bad. We don't know the satisfaction a meal brings unless we know what hunger is. We don't know the pleasure of warmth if we have not experienced cold. The absence of hugs and sexual satisfaction drives us to pursue it. Not having something makes us appreciate it when we get to have it.

Not having love in our hearts drive us to find ways to feel it and enjoy it.

Depressive states of our minds are like barometers of the level of love we operate from. When we run low on love, we get mental fog, and life seems to become harder. People around us seem to treat us unfairly. Our physical body seems to work against us. They are all signs of focusing on the opposite of what love is, not on what brings us joy. That is why all the religions and philosophies of the world tell us that love is the only important objective to strive towards.

What We Judge in Others, We Judge in Ourselves

Love feels good. Hope feels good. Appreciation feels good. Gratitude feels good. Anger, hate, revenge, frustration and sadness do not feel good.

There is nothing wrong with any of those emotions – they are there to make us realise where we are, to show us what lessons about life we have yet to learn. Like hunger and satisfaction from a meal, we need to feel hunger to move towards finding food for our bodies. When we feel disappointment or anger towards others, it is the life force telling us that we need to look for love to conquer those.

Finding love after feeling heavy from the emotion of anger feels like sipping water after being very thirsty. It makes us present. It makes us appreciate what we needed to continue. Finding food and water after experiencing hunger and thirst makes us realise how important both of those are to our physical existence. Searching for and finding love after feeling upset, empty and angry is healing to our souls and minds.

We do not get angry at food or water for not being there to save us from starvation. We appreciate it when we find it and enjoy it. When we find joy in living, when we heal our hearts after choosing love, why do we blame those who allowed us to look for it, to start appreciating the peace of mind that loving gives us?

Those who made us have the tough lessons about love are put on the path of our journey for that reason. To teach us to love. The love that encompasses everything. Not the one-sided one. Not the one that says, "unless you behave in a way that pleases me, I will not accept you and will not love you."

The love that only truly matters is the one that allows us to see ourselves as the reflection of everyone around us, without taking any parts off or adding any.

We were made as a reflection of our creator, whether that is God or the universe, and they are perfection. So are we, every single one of us.

That is why when we feel that we are not good enough, for whatever reason, we feel uneasiness in our minds and stomachs. Because we are denying God's perfection. We are shrinking in our magnificence instead of celebrating it. When we look at someone around us and say that they need to change for us to accept them and love them, we say to our creator, that he has made a mistake.

That is the reason why criticism and putting ourselves above others in our judgments does not feel good. Eventually, it will create physical symptoms in our body to try to teach us to love. Anything that we judge in others, we judge in ourselves. We are not kind to ourselves when we point fingers at others. It means we are pointing it at ourselves.

Love Heals

Love heals. Love wants to be present in our hearts. Love will fight the battles in our minds to bring us back to balance anytime when we get off the track.

Where there is love, there is joy. Joy is our natural state of being. Joy makes us present with others and makes us present and connected to us. A state of joy is where creation happens.

I have learned then when my perceptions of others bring me down, I should look for something that will bring me back to be present and joyful. Any time when fear, anxiety or anger comes because of thinking that I am missing out on something, or that someone has treated me unfairly, I start calming my thoughts by putting them on paper.

I would write what made me upset or worried. That way I put it down instead of having it floating in my head. After some time of chewing on it, I will try to balance those thoughts by stacking positives against the negatives that I perceive.

Every event becomes neutral once we stack enough positives against perceived negatives. I look for blessings in every crisis. When it is not easy to do it quickly in my head, I would sit down and start writing the blessings down. Whenever I had anger or judgment sitting with me for too long, I would make myself write from 100 to 500 benefits. It is amazing how transforming that is. It does not have to be that many, about 20 will already start to remould our minds, but I usually like to push myself to have the results faster and have them ingrained in my mind.

Our sadness and depression live in our heads – those are the thoughts that we keep repeating to ourselves that keep us stuck and trapped in the prison that we hold the key to.

I used to imagine myself sitting in a cold, dark prison cell that I have created inside of my heart by blaming others. I put myself there voluntarily and put others there with me. I would imagine myself sitting there in a dark corner and clenching the key in my hand. I had the choice to open it up and see the sunshine, to hug my loved ones and receive love, but I would choose not to. I would tell myself that I can let go of those thoughts that were keeping me there. My mind would argue with me that it is the others who keep me there. So, for the time being, I would let it go and try again later, to convince myself that I do hold the key to my freedom.

In Love with the Moon and the Universe

Every emotion has a frequency. Everything in us and around us is a vibration. When we choose an emotion, we choose the frequency. I used to be fascinated by physics, wanted to understand what is making this world go around and what are the rules of nature, and which applies to us humans, as we are part of nature and the universe. As a teenager, I used to come out at night and stare at the sky.

My grandparents' house in the country was perfect for stargazing. It seemed as if there was life out there, and the thousand-star lights represented the lights from the many houses up there. The most puzzling part was the idea that we live on a round ball called Earth, and we are not attached to anything, just floating in space. I could not get my head around that idea. It seemed that we are just so small in that vast universe.

While that concept was reassuring to me that we are not just those simple beings meant to just sleep, eat and worry about simple things, I was convinced that we are created by something with amazing power. There had to be more to us than what we could see.

The moon was my favourite. I loved staring at it when it was full. From the place where I would observe it, in the northern hemisphere in southern Poland, I could see a face on it. It had eyes and a mouth. It was a bit tilted, but it always looked at me. The moon became my friend. I felt safe and felt like I belonged during those nights when I would look up and admire the magnificence of that big, shiny ball so far away.

That is probably where my beliefs in all kinds of possibilities and even far-fetched fairy tales have come from. Something inside me was connecting with me and telling me that there is so much more to life than we know.

Yet, I felt disconnected from most of the people I was meeting during my life. I loved being surrounded by people, but for the most part, there was not much that I wanted to talk to them about. Most of them did not know me, and I would get bored with different groups of people easily. It felt as I was wasting my time somehow, or as if they did not see me for who I was.

When I was young, the only person that I felt connected to was my Babcia, my grandmother from my mum's side. She loved me unconditionally and I loved her back with all my heart.

I visited her as often as I could when I lived in Poland. The way she always looked at me and spoke to me was full of acceptance and understanding. Her stories from the time of war made for many interesting conversations. Her strength and how she would overcome challenges inspired me to never give up and make her proud.

Seeing the Light

While I was still living in my fantasy land, believing that my husband would come back, I started looking for love from other men. One of my closest friends invited me to my favourite place, where there was music and dancing. Music and dancing were always my companions and an escape. As a teenager, I would never pass up an opportunity to dance. Music will soothe and fill my soul with calmness and take me to beautiful places that only certain rhythms will awake. I forget myself in a dance to good music.

It was the end of April, more than two years since I was on my own, and my best friend was singing in my favourite bar. She called and invited me to come. I said yes but freaked out later and felt that I could not face walking in there on my own. The depressive state had sucked out all the confidence from me. I was a shaking mess when I tried to go to public places, and this time it was the same. I called half of the dozens of my girlfriends, asking if they would join me, but everyone was busy. I did not want to disappoint my friend, so I put myself together and decided to go, to have a glass of wine and then come back home.

After arriving, I met my friend's husband and he invited me to his table that was positioned in the middle of the bar. The place was full and very loud, which was good because I could just blend in.

My friend did not have time for me, as she was the singer in the band, but I met some of her friends. Paula was one of them. She was super friendly and become my companion for the night. The music was great, the dancing gave me the high that took me away from my worries and to a land where everything was perfect and there were no worries.

Paula and I started chatting with a young man next to us. He was Italian, which I liked because I could impress him with my knowledge of his language. He was tall, good looking and charming. The three of us were having a great time, talking, drinking and dancing. He kept ordering jugs of sangria, and I tried to say that I could not drink much because I needed to drive later, but he insisted and proposed that if I got too drunk, he would take me home in a taxi. I had not had that much fun in ages. The Spanish music that I loved, fun friends and a handsome Italian all felt like a dream.

At some stage, I asked Paula if she liked him, as we were all chatting and dancing together. She said that she was married and if I liked him that I should keep partying with him.

His name was Marco – the name I wanted to give my son since it was one of my favourite male Italian names. He was funny and smart. We sat outside and talked about books and poetry. He was also more than ten years younger than me. That did not matter. I was not looking for a partner, I was looking for attention, and I got plenty of it. We drank sangria, we danced, we talked, we laughed.

When the music stopped around midnight, one of my new friends that I met that night offered to drive us home. We dropped Marco off at his motel, then she dropped me off. Before I said goodbye to Marco, he said that he will pick me up the next day and take me out for breakfast, then we could pick up my car. I liked that idea but was not counting on it. He was charming but I thought that he was not that interested in me, and we all had a few drinks by then. I was hoping to see him again.

Looking for Acceptance

The night that I had just had in his company was magic. It felt so good to act and feel normal, even if it did not last long. I was not overthinking it, but I was enjoying every moment while it lasted.

Back at the house, I kept thinking about my husband again and how much I missed him. The place was quiet, dark, and empty. The children usually spent the weekends at their dad's because they would work on weekend nights and Sundays.

The loneliness felt so overwhelming, and I would try to switch my mind off from sad thoughts by cuddling up to the pillows on the couch in our lounge, trying to fall to sleep. Those couches saw so many happy moments with children's laughter, family times and friends around.

The past that I missed and the future that I had hoped for and imagined were being erased by the present situation that I found myself in. I felt lots of pain for the children. I had no answers for them. The mother that they knew was no more. The mother that they needed was not there either. I have tried to shelter them as much as I could from what I was experiencing and what I was going through, but there is not much that you can hide when you are not able to even look after yourself.

Around midday, Isabella, who gave us a lift home the night before and who I had just met the night before, came over to visit and see if I would need a ride to get my car. I had not heard from Marco during the day, so I was happy that she offered to help. My children were staying with their dad for another night. While I was chatting with Isabella, I got a text from Marco saying that if I am available, he wants to pick me up and take me out for dinner.

That was a very nice surprise. He did not forget, he did enjoy our evening together, and he wanted to take me out on a date!

I felt a bit like the 17-year-old me. He arrived while Isabella was still in my place. I was excited and nervous at the same time. I wanted to leave the house with Marco as soon as I could, but Isabella was enjoying chatting with him. At last, we left and took off in his work Ute.

He proposed we go to Cape Hillsborough and have some dinner there. By the time we arrived, it was dark. The corner store where they served meals was open, but the kitchen was already closed. We were able to only buy some dry chips and soft drinks.

Marco suggested eating at the beach. He pulled out a rug from the back of his Ute and we found a nice spot on the beach. It was one of those nights when the moon was almost full. The ocean waves were reflecting its light beautifully, the sky was full of stars.

The scene was like from a movie: the beach, the waves, the moon, two people who had just met and wondering where the evening is going to take them.

The New Me That I Met That Night

Previously, before I got married, whenever I was on dates I would overthink everything. I would worry about how I look, if he likes me and what I should or should not do when things got intimate.

This time I was mostly in disbelief that it was happening.

It was like I had been kidnapped by aliens, taken to a tropical Island, put on the beach and the moon was installed to reflect the silver of the calm ocean. Then those aliens put next to me a man that looked like a Greek God, with his muscular body, charming smile, and intellect of Mark Aurelius. Movies are made of that stuff, and I was playing the starring role in this one.

I was truly in the clouds, just gazing at the stars and the ocean, while he kissed my neck and touched me softly. Could it get any better? It did!

We left our blanket and our belongings and decided to go for a walk along the beach. I took my jeans off to not make them wet. The night was hot, the water temperature perfect for a dip. We walked into the ocean and sat just deep enough to have half of our bodies submerged. He took his clothes off, then took mine off. We were sitting in the water facing each other, our legs around each other's bodies. I touched his chest and told him how he reminded me of the statues of Greek gods that I remembered visiting in museums in Florence.

We kissed, hugged and touched each other. Life does stop in those moments. For me, it was so important because it was the touch of a man that I craved so much. And it was not just any touch. I craved the touch of the man that used to touch me, and I used to love it. I had occasionally had one-night dates but was not interested in it.

This time with Marco, it was different. I wanted it because we did not want anything else from each other. Neither of us were looking for love or a relationship. Just the pure pleasure of kisses, touch and the excitement that comes with it.

When we started to walk back, we were both naked. He said that I had a beautiful body and that he was impressed that I was so confident to walk naked beside him. After he said it, I thought to myself that I did not feel embarrassed at all, that I did feel proud of my body and proud of myself for allowing myself to be in a moment and enjoying it.

That was not the usual me. I was the kind of lover who liked the lights off, who would keep my eyes closed, who was not brave enough to ask for what I wanted where lovemaking was concerned. I would worry about other's pleasure, and not know how to put into words what would give me pleasure. My husband was a great lover, always hungry for sex, any time and any place. I was not starved of good sex, but I was not brave enough to ask for what I liked.

While we walked along the beach, some people passed us. We could see each other in the light from the moon. We laughed, as we were both naked, but it did not matter to us. Back on the blanket, we kept kissing and cuddling. It was a night to remember.

The next day he was being transferred to Rockhampton for work. He took me to the place where I had left my car the night before and we said our goodbyes.

Crossing the Bridge

It looked like the heavens had opened above my head. Small rays of sunshine were getting through, and the warmth was melting the ice around my heart, the ice that kept it frozen and unable to feel that I can be loved again.

I knew in my mind that I could try to forget my husband, but every attempt to do so was taken out by the pain of missing him and not knowing how I could love anyone so much again.

The fairy tale with Marco continued for almost four months. He would come to Mackay for work and stay in hotels. We would go out, then spend the evenings together. There were many beautiful moments when we would roll on the beach, get covered in sand or get bitten by mosquitos. Moments of making love in my car, or just kissing passionately on the streets. It was a road for me to forget my past and look into the future. He once put it beautifully and metaphorically: "I am the bridge for you." He was a bridge that took me over to the other side.

I took a plane trip to Rockhampton to visit him, we met on the Gold Coast, and I enjoyed staying in the

Sofitel overlooking the Surfers Paradise beach. We talked about life and philosophies, but it was never going anywhere and it ended leaving me with some great memories.

He was a perfect gentleman with me, and I will always be thankful to him for taking me over that bridge and to the other side. From the old island of my life where my life had happened until then, to the new one that had much more to offer.

He was also an answer to my wish for a man that I asked for at that time. In my diaries I wrote all the details I wanted in a man. Somehow, I wrote the description *younger*. I'm not sure why. One month after writing it, I met him.

Books That Would Talk to Me

Marco bought me a beautiful book that he had ordered for me: *Jonathan Livingston Seagull* by Richard Bach.

It is the story of a bird that breaks from his flock and flies higher than others thought possible. Some of my favourite lines from that book are:

"Break the chains of your thought, and you break the chains of your body, too."

"To fly as fast as thought, to anywhere that is ... you must begin by knowing that you have already arrived..."

"The trick was to know that his true nature lived, as perfect as an unwritten number, anywhere at once across space and time."

I have always looked for a deeper meaning in everything that I see and experience, and with this book, it was not only significant that Marco was as deep a thinker as I was, but also gifted me a book about expanding our views about life, a book that shows us that we can rise above our limitations. The book states that if we can conceive something as a thought, to experience it is a possibility, that is as real as the thought. I have proven it to myself by wanting many things and experiences and having them come true.

Another significant sign for me was that my husband had only owned one book, apart from his cooking books. That book was given to him by a girl that he met in Scilly, while he was living and working there. I think that she liked him. In Italian, it is called *Il Gabbiano Jonathan Livingston.*

The date under the dedication is 26.08.1994. I met him a few days later when he moved from Falcone in Sicily to Fie Allo Sciliar in the Italian Alps.

These were the two significant Italian men in my life. The first came to my life with that book, and stayed by my side from 1994 till 2012, 18 years. The second stayed for four months and gifted me this book during our last meeting.

Coincidence? Or is the Universe sending me messages and I'm taking time to read them? I love finding meaning in everything in my life, and I also love creating my destiny, and with both I believe I have brought them to my life because I have wished for them.

They represented what I have asked for and delivered some experiences and lessons that I maybe was not fully aware that I wanted. From the perspective of time and the knowledge I have now, I know that I have asked for those lessons. Every single one of them. Somewhere in my subconscious, I was wrestling with those questions about the meaning of life, what love truly is, why we feel dissatisfied even when we have lots, and so on.

We think that life is testing us or punishing us when we encounter people or circumstances that are challenging or hurtful towards us. I understood that whatever is doing it to us, God, the Higher Mind, Universe, or nature, is 100 % on our side. It would not give us something that we have not somehow conceived in our minds first. Someone may argue that if that was so why will small children have challenges that they cannot contemplate yet.

I believe that they came to this life knowing what they want to accomplish, and to be able to live the life they want and to understand life, they need to have those challenges.

Loving the Lessons I Did Not Want to Learn

I would never have understood the meaning of what love is if I had not gone through the experience of hurting from love and wanting for love so much as if my breath and life depended on it.

I could have read what it is, what it feels like to love, but to know, to feel the depth of love, is only possible if we know what it is to fight for it, to go to the end of the world to find it. Everyone in their lifetime will be put into situations where they can find that kind of love. To have it, to lose it, to feel the beauty of it, to be deeply hurt by it.

Some will dust themselves off from those perceived hurts and love even more, love without limits, share the love and never look back. Some will crumble and see the hurts only as hurts, not as what they truly are: the lessons of love. Those individuals will keep getting those lessons over and over, and the opportunity to love will be forever present.

They will try to tell themselves that their love is enough for them, that they are not interested in more, but their soul will not give up, and the thirst for the experience of pure love will make them keep searching.

Neither are better off in life. A journey is a journey. We keep going forward, one step at a time, one minute at a time, one breath at a time. The ones who have made peace with their "hurts" by being thankful for them will have more freedom because their thirst for the answers will be quenched to some extent.

The ones who will see life as black and white, wanted and unwanted, nice and mean, will run towards certain people and away from certain people. They will trust less and be afraid more, but nonetheless, they will have their understanding of life and support from the Universe that will carry them through.

Part Summary – Key Points

1. Write your worries down: putting it on paper helps to narrow it down.

   List enough benefits to every crisis so it becomes neutral in your mind and reduces the stress levels.

   Emotions have frequencies, so choose the thoughts and actions that make you feel good.

2. We attract from a place of faith or fear.

   As fear is the stronger emotions, we create the unwanted.

   The more we are grateful for, the more we get to be grateful for.

3. No-one is faithful to us - everyone is faithful to their values. We attract what we need to learn.

   We attract partners and friends according to the level of our self-confidence.

Part 4:
Love, Loss and Hope

Finding the Answers

I spent the whole of 2014 picking up the pieces of what was left of me. I had been on my own for three years, and my decision to search and find answers to life's biggest questions was starting to bring long-awaited rewards.

I read lots of books from different writers. I attended seminars that were packed with knowledge and wisdom run by the Demartini Institute: the signature Breakthrough Experience; The Prophecy; The Mastery of Life. I enrolled on a Facilitators Training Program in the coming year.

That investment has given me the knowledge I needed to restore my faith in people. It gave me the tools for life, and it gave me the biggest gift: the belief that there was nothing wrong with me, and more than that, it helped me to realise my own magnificence.

With that, I have learned how amazing and perfect everyone around me is, and how the universe is built and run with a precision that even our unlimited mind has trouble comprehending. I have learned that my purpose on Earth is to connect with others, while we are all looking for answers and gift each other the wisdom that we all have been born with.

I met many interesting people and stayed in touch with many of them. I chose coaches that have guided me to the shores when I was getting too deep into my version of a perceived victim of other's actions. One of which was a male coach, who would coach me through Skype. I was having a hard time dealing with an issue of a financial nature that had to do with my ex. It was very frustrating and upsetting at the time. He gave me an exercise: write up to 200 benefits to having that "problem" present in my life.

It is hard to see positives to something that is causing us stress, but I knew that it was a way to get me out of my head and to mental stability. In those times when we are convinced that we are not treated fairly it is not easy to see.

His words of advice were that this situation, as all before them, will pass. Anything that we encounter in life, good or bad, will pass. But, if we are not grateful for everything in life, as if it was the best thing that has happened to us, then we will repeat that lesson until we see that everything that happens to us is a blessing. He proceeded to say that my situation will be resolved because everything is with time, but because of my unbalanced perceptions about it (that I was perceiving it as a crisis) I would attract that lesson again. That could be in my relationships, health or vocation.

His advice stuck with me. I knew that what I was experiencing I have created. I lived in fear, not with faith. Whatever we fear, we attract.

I did not want to recreate another lack of something or problems in other areas of my life, so that night I found and wrote more than 200 benefits to the financial crisis. Once I started, it was very easy. There were so many benefits in all areas of my life. I will be forever grateful to all the coaches that I have met and who have shared their gifts with me to open my eyes to what I was blind to. As the greatest minds have wisely observed, they can take our freedom away, they can cut off parts of our body, but no one can take away our love and wisdom. That is why it is important to invest in ourselves and keep acquiring the wisdom that is out there and keep cultivating the love in our hearts. Those two, our *love* and our *wisdom* can never be taken away from us.

Breaking the Fantasy of What Love is

During my studies with Dr John Demartini, he would explain that when we are in love, it is when we are elated by it and become blind to the downsides of someone; depression is the other side, when we are blind to the upsides of our situation.

The elation and the depression both create a fantasy in our minds so we see experiences as one-sided events only. The two are opposite to each other. Being in love and elated makes us want something because we perceive it to have mostly positives that we are attracted to. Being depressed and anxious makes us try to avoid and run away from something because we perceive that it has more negatives.

At the time of my marriage breaking up I was like a pendant swinging from being elated and wanting him back, creating a fantasy of how good my life with him was, to being depressed and creating a fantasy of how awful my life will be in the future without him.

When I was first told that my depression was a fantasy that I have created in my mind and chose to hold onto, I did believe it was the case. I am a logical thinker, and anything that I can see an order to, will convince me. I am deeply spiritual in my beliefs as well, but only if an idea has a logical basis.

I was hurting from my self-induced love state and depressive state, but the explanation from Dr Demartini's teachings was making sense to me like nothing before, so I made a promise to myself to break that fantasy and be well again. I understood that we cannot blame ourselves while looking back, thinking that we could have acted differently or been more of something or less of something. We are perfect as we are, nothing to add, nothing to take out.

It is our task in life to work on understanding and accepting other's behaviour towards us, and not to make others happy or deal with their anger or other issues. This separation of tasks, as one of the philosophers nicely put it, made me understand that it is not our fault if others are angry with us; it is their task to work out why they have that reaction. When someone is upset with us, we help them learn to love.

The way that I was angry with my ex-husband showed me that. His behaviour made me choose to look for answers to my anger, and, in turn, made me find a way to turn that anger into a love for him. If it was not for his behaviours that first made me angry, I would have never decided to work on myself and to find what love is.

Having someone angry at us gives them an amazing opportunity to work on themselves. They may choose the easy road and keep blaming us for how they feel, or maybe in time, they will realise our contribution to their growth. Either way, it is their task and their choice.

New Job, New Me

I was on the road to reclaiming my life. My head was still full of brain noise that I was a victim of someone else's actions, my emotions were swinging from very down to up when I would practice my gratitude tasks that I have been learning. I was probably a case of a bipolar person to my children, but I was getting back to normal.

2012 was the darkest year, 2013 was marked by the suffering of my sister and the death of hopes to resurrect my marriage when solicitors got involved, 2014 was the one when I would step outside of the house and face the world, meet new people, have a go at dating as well as invest in myself and study the rules about life.

At the end of November 2014, after applying for many different jobs and not getting a single interview, I was asked to attend one for a position in the bar in an Aero Club.

I was scared but hoping that I made a good impression. I had my favourite red, black and white dress on. It was elegant and a little sexy at the same time. I walked to that lonely building in an area of town that I did not know existed. A tall man was standing in the bar with his back to me. I said hi and he greeted me with a welcoming smile. It was a good start. He invited me to sit down for a chat in the far corner of the club. The interview was very informal: he was impressed with my experience and said that I was probably overqualified for the position of a bar person. I told him that it was perfect for me and told him a bit about my private situation. He was pleased that I was a mature person and from Europe. He was born in Austria. Speaking to him was very easy – he was very polite, funny and good looking. I got the job and was super happy that I would start earning money and that my boss was such a nice person.

I started in January, just two days a week, and sometimes on the weekend if there was a function booked. I was only getting around ten hours a week, but I was happy to take it slow. The work was easy and the people who ran it were very welcoming and helpful. My boss became my friend and would often help me out behind the bar if it got busy, and he was always there if I needed anything. After every shift we would sit down and chat. Other club members would sometimes stay as well and join us. I loved that I was appreciated and liked at the club, and that I had a great relationship with him. His position at the club, the same as other members, was voluntary. He was the secretary at the time but was always there when it was open. He would come straight after his day job, often still wearing his orange uniform. I found him very good looking and very smart. He seemed to know everything about everything and was always happy to talk with me. He got to know my story and was very supportive.

I did not know much about him. He did not talk about himself or his family. He loved talking about his life in Europe before he emigrated to Australia in the eighties. We were connecting most while talking about how much we missed Europe.

This new friendship and having a job helped to regain my confidence. It was great to be liked and know that I could be a valuable worker. Since my ex-husband and I had our businesses for the whole duration of my marriage, I did not work anywhere else. I forgot how great I could be at any work that I decide to do. Having customers loving my service and employers happy with my work ethic helped to lift me and give me that much-needed fuel to rebuild myself.

Being the "Wrong Energy"

Since starting my studies of the nature of life and the workings of the human mind and body in 2014, I was building the foundation to restarting my life in all areas.

My finances were still tied up with my husband, and we were still officially married. There was no agreement when it came to sharing the care of the children, as all the attempts to communicate in person or through any agencies were rejected by my ex. He truly lived by the belief that I was the devil energy that his new group was embracing in their teachings.

Our children were given special cards from him, blessed by the spiritual leader of his group, that were put under their beds to protect them from the bad energies around them. It was upsetting me when the children would do that just to please their dad. He was installing fear in them that they are sources of badness around them, and especially in our home.

I believed the opposite, that there is only love around us and in others who are around us. Some of the people who got hurt by that group and the families who were divided by them were in touch with me, and I knew that they were powerful and there was no chance of having any kind of relationship with my ex if those people had their grip on him.

I was vindicated when his group was exposed by the media with many examples of them spreading their new beliefs and putting fear in their followers that they would suffer in the afterlife unless they follow them and be part of their teaching, following their leader who had “special powers”. Their leader has accumulated millions of dollars here and overseas and runs his organization as a charity to avoid taxes. They refused to talk to any press or media while being exposed as one of the cults in Australia at the time. Even our local paper had stories about their involvement in breaking up families.

That was the hardest part of coming to terms with my new life. I was not able to have any answers for my children, for their day-to-day life because we as parents were not communicating at all. They were moving from my house to his every week, as well as sleeping extra nights at his place due to working at night at his business. I had no say if I wanted to have all the children with me for a single weekend. He would get angry with them if they would try to avoid work and, not wanting to face that anger, did as he wanted.

I did not have the strength or the heart to fight to have them with me for the full week. I did not want them to be in the middle of that. The only subject that was vital to me was that they kept attending the school that they started from kindergarten. That was their wish as well.

The Mentor Who Asked the Right Questions

I lived trying to follow the philosophy of seeing the balance in everything, trying to be grateful for everything that is happening to me and around me.

After restarting my studies and attending seminars, I also had a one-on-one meeting with the founder of the Demartini Institute in November 2014, Dr John Demartini. It was not easy to get an appointment with him, and it was very expensive, but I was lucky to get one and able to borrow the money from my niece.

I had only one hour with him, and I had so many questions. I was still hurting a lot from losing my husband, and I had lots of anger towards him for his conduct towards me and was living with anxiety about the future. I arrived in Brisbane and had the meeting in one of the hotels there.

That one hour has been very beneficial to my recovery and turned my life around much faster. In that one hour, he helped me to see all my problems from different angles. I wanted help with healing my heart and freedom from gripping fear.

He has asked me what is it that I am missing the most. I told him that it was not having my best friend next to me, not sharing intimate moments with him, not having the unit of the family as well as the financial stability that we had achieved and was now lost.

He proceeded to tell me that nothing is ever missing, it just changes form. When I focus on having something in just one form, then I would feel the void of it, but nature does not allow for anything to be missing. It is only our perception of not having something and our inability to recognise it in other forms.

To my problem of not having my husband in my life anymore, as my partner, as my friend, and as my lover, Dr Demartini asked who has taken on that role now. The new form could be in just one person or many. He asked who specifically has taken on those roles.

I had to admit that I had become closer with a few friends that were there for me as a good partner would be, and I was able to count on them and be myself with them. Love was also aplenty, my children would hug me more, would tell me that they loved me. Close friends have repeatedly told me that I am loved and appreciated. Some male friends would visit me frequently, offering help around the house or taking me out. I would notice other men's interest in me when in the shops.

I was shown that the missing part of having a friend and a lover was transformed onto other people who were gathering around me. I was not alone, but I was supported, I was loved, I was wanted.

Regarding financial support, I would recognise how my friends have been bringing me food, how my children have started being resourceful and finding ways to live with less money. My new form of having finances was living off the savings, and he asked me to find benefits to that new form.

Having more attention and closer bonds with my girlfriends and with male friends, as well as being closer with the children, has had the benefit of knowing that it was genuine. They all were there for me because they wanted to be. There was no hidden agenda with it, just pure care and love to support me. I was surrounded by so much more love than if it was coming just from one person.

Then I was asked what the drawbacks would be, the negative aspects if I was still receiving the attention and love from my husband. I had to admit that when I was being loved and supported by my husband, I was often put in a situation where I would act as he wanted, not what I wanted, to please him. I was afraid of losing his approval and love. With the love and support I was getting from my friends and children, I was not in any way worried that I could lose that love.

I saw that the new form was there, and it was much better for me. It was an eye-opener. I had heard before that nothing is ever missing, but have not done the exercise to look for the new forms.

With the financial issue, the benefits to the new form of financial support were having the freedom to decide what I buy without having to ask anyone for permission.

Dr Demartini has also helped me to heal the pain of knowing that my husband was with a new partner. He has pointed out that there were benefits for me because of her presence in his life. I could not see any, but he did not give up until I could see it. I saw that her being in his life was giving me the push to move on, and the permission to start having serious interests in potential partners without guilt. It set me free from holding on to the hope that he will come back, and that we could restore our marriage and family.

Finding the Balance that Healed My Mind

At the time of that meeting, I was not free from the anxiety or pain inside of me, but everything he said and finding the benefits to all the perceived negatives and seeing the new forms made so much sense to me. My heart responds to logic. I do not believe in something just because someone says it is true. Instead, my mind goes into research mode to see if what I hear has enough substance and if there is evidence to it.

With what I was presented during my meeting, there was nothing that I could argue with. The questions were simple, and the answers were mine. I could see how my mind had been unbalanced, seeing only what I was missing out on instead of seeing also what I was gaining in the absence of the old form.

Since then, I have learned that it is the new form that I wanted more than the old one. The subconscious mind has been brewing what I wanted for a while and has pushed me towards that what I truly want.

I was, without realising it, wishing to be loved differently, wishing to be able to be more open in a relationship, wishing to be more seen and heard.

It was not his doing; it was the universe just answering my calling for experiences that would teach me how to love, experiences that would take me on the journey to meet people who would appreciate me and everything that I represent, and the possibility to live with without fear or guilt. Freedom was the gift that I have received from having those experiences, The freedom to know that whatever I do or do not do, I am worthy of love because there are benefits to others from all my actions.

Freedom from a fear that if something was missing from my life, I would suffer. I know now that the new form will appear.

Freedom from the guilt that I did something wrong or did not do something, knowing that all things are two-sided, so no one can miss out on anything. If I was not there for someone, a new person would step in and provide the balance.

I finished my meeting with John with a promise to write a thank you letter to my still husband and his partner, listing everything that I have perceived missing, listing new forms and the benefits to those new forms. The thank you letter was not for them to read, but for me to write so I can name what I perceived as being one-sided, and how them doing what they did was a blessing to my life.

Gratitude is not the positive feeling of being thankful for something that we like. To feel true gratitude is to see both sides of an event and be thankful for the experience. I was lucky to learn that technique and have felt the gratitude deep in my heart. Gratitude and appreciation for life as it is, for everyone as they are, is the message that I would love to be able to spread to the world. The hunger for knowing how to acquire the ability to keep finding gratitude is my life's mission, and to be able to explain and teach gratitude is the reason I wanted to tell my story.

The Sky Fell Down on Me Again

In February 2013, one year after the start of the collapse of my marriage and seeing that my ex-husband was not interested in me at all, was when I first started looking for work.

My mum was with me, and she was a great help. Just having someone who cared next to me every day was a blessing. The children had cooked meals again and the love from their grandma. She did not speak English, but she had a great relationship with my children, and they understood each other very well.

Looking for work proved to be very difficult for me. Not working for any other business except ours had left me with limited qualifications and very low self-esteem. I have not seen myself as an asset to any business. Being a full-time mum for fourteen years has made me doubt myself and my abilities, and being constantly anxious has not helped either. I was scared, very scared.

I would drive to some businesses, park nearby and sit in the car for over an hour, often crying because I felt so little. Then I would go in, leave my resume and walk away as quickly as I could.

I got invited for an interview for the position of a support worker. I passed and was offered a position. I had volunteering experience from my time in Poland, caring for people with different disabilities.

Two weeks after starting my new job, I got a phone call from my sister Ania in Poland. Our younger sister was in the hospital. She was admitted a few days before with back pain and was going in for MRI scans, and because her body was shaking so badly, she was given an injection. When she came out, she was paralysed from the neck down. The diagnosis was stage four cancer. The doctors could not do anything else for her, and the decision was made to send her to the hospice until she died. I asked to speak to her, but Ania said that she was so distressed and could not talk to me or our mum.

The sky was falling on me again. One year after a tragedy, a new one started unfolding. My mum was devastated. While she was in Australia trying to save one daughter, the other was literally dying. I could not believe why it all was happening around me, but in some selfish way, I was thinking that I could escape my pain at home and go to Poland with mum to try to help my sister.

I made lots of phone calls to people in Poland, asking for medical help for my sister. I did not want to think that there was nothing that could be done. Many people wanted to help but did not know how. I also called my Polish friend from Budapest, whose partner had connections to the Polish government.

She happened to be on a ski lift in Italy but picked up my call and offered to help.

My husband was very kind at that time. He helped me to organise a ticket and gave me some cash from the business as spending money. The night before our trip, after my asking, he made love to me. Everything was happening again like in a movie that I was an actress in. They say that God never puts us through something that we are not able to handle, and when it is too hard to go through something, he does not walk beside us. Instead, he carries us.

The coming months felt like that for me. I was carried by God. I was in his strong hands. I was supported and guided. Otherwise, I don't know how I would have survived it.

My husband moved back to our house to take care of the children. I was so happy about that and imagined the tragedy of my sister's illness as a helping hand in my marriage.

Fighting for My Sister's Life

While we were on the plane to Poland, my sister was being transported to a specialist hospital in another town, to be operated on. My friends' partner was able to get in touch with someone high up who authorised the operation. I was very happy about that and hopeful that we could save her life. At the same time, while up high in the sky, I and mum kept praying that she would survive the operation, and that we would see her again.

That beautiful Polish friend of mine, Ula, lived in Budapest and in Italy. We met in Australia. She arrived five years before in Cairns with a group of Italian tourists that were visiting my in-laws. We liked each other straight away. At the time I was immersed in a study about relationships with the Demartini Institute, and she loved all the knowledge that I had and wanted to learn from me. She came and visited us the year after and stayed for two months.

I love meeting new people, and love cultivating friendships. Once again, I was given an example that everything we do for others comes back to us multiplied.

After arriving in Poland, my sister's ex-husband drove me and her thirteen-year-old daughter to the town where the operation was taking place.

It was heart-breaking to see my sister lying in a hospital bed, unable to move any part of her body except her head. The good news was that since she had the operation, the pain in her neck was gone, and there was hope that she could be treated and recover. I held on to that hope every day for the coming weeks.

I organised a rehabilitation for my sister and a transfer to a good private clinic. She was very upbeat and convinced that she could get better. Most of the doctors were not giving us much good news, but I was not giving up. I was by her bedside every day. She could not drink without help, she could not adjust her pillow without help, she could not do anything. I fed her, talked with her, was by her side all day every day, but mostly I was doing everything I could to keep the hope alive.

She went from the specialist hospital back to our town hospital, and from there to the rehabilitation clinic. She was getting better there, and I fought for her and organised a transfer to an oncology hospital.

The night before the transfer, we received a phone call that she was taken into hospital because she had started bleeding. Mum and I picked up a taxi and travelled through the town to that hospital. It was the middle of the night, and it felt as if the sky was falling on top of us again.

When we arrived, the doctors were attending to my sister. We were waiting in the hall, but I could catch a glimpse of her looking at me with tears and fear in her eyes. I think she was devastated that she could not do better, that she could not be stronger and that her body was giving up on her. I was fighting so hard for her to get her help, but she probably felt that she was letting me down.

I will never forget that look on her face, that fear and pain, paralysed, and unable to do anything.

Trying Not to Give Up

In my moments of panic, trouble and frustration with life, I would remind myself how much my sister dealt with. Remembering it helps me to wake myself up from my moments of self-pity and reminds me how lucky I am.

I have always had the fortune of a healthy body. I could hug the people I wanted, I could lift a cup of tea and I could go where I wanted. She could not. Later, the ability to talk was taken away from her as well. But she never gave up.

That day, the doctors were able to stop the bleeding, but she was not in a good way. After a few days, she was released from hospital and sent home. There was nothing more than they could do for her. She came home where neither myself nor my mum knew how to take care of her. It was good to be able to have her close, but we were both struggling to give her the care that was needed. I was making phone calls every day and trying to find a hospital that would agree to treat her.

One night when, as usual, my sister was not sleeping, I went to check on her and found that she was in a pool of blood. Mum and I tried to clean it up and ended up with a bucket full of blood that was coming out of her. We were all terrified. When the ambulance arrived, we were told that she was very close to dying from blood loss. She was taken to yet another hospital, the sixth in three months, and had a blood transfusion.

I was not giving up, and every morning I would try to gather the strength to face a new day. I would lie down in bed with my eyes closed and tell myself that everything is happening for a reason and that I can handle what the day will bring.

The strange thing was that I was still in lots of pain from not being able to talk to my husband as I used to, that he still was as distant as ever and that our marriage was falling apart. I communicated with the children on Skype. They were missing me terribly but were very understanding. We would talk in the morning, while it was the afternoon in Australia. I was fearful for my family, and sometimes lost strength and hope while caring for my sister.

The children so often became my counsellors, talking calmly while I was sobbing , telling me that they are strong, doing what they need to and they know that I have the strength to keep going and support my sister. From far away, they were the angels that were holding me up so I would not fall.

Climbing Mount Everest Together

After attending a private consultation with an oncologist, the young doctor agreed to organise a meeting for me with a couple of specialists in the hospital where he worked.

I was not able to have my sister with me during the visit, as she could only travel by ambulance. I waited for hours until they would hear me out.

They looked over the papers and told me that it is stage four cancer, and the chances were slim, but because my sister was young (she was 44), they agreed to admit her and to start radiation therapy for her.

It was another small win. While spending many hours at the many hospitals, we were meeting lots of doctors, nurses and patients. We were told so often by them that they were amazed at how close a bond we had. They were in disbelief that I would sit by her side all day every day, and that we would smile and be so upbeat all the time.

I would read to Dorka. I love reading and wanted to read to her lots of words of love and hope. One of the books, by Rhonda Byrne, was called *The Power* and it was our favourite, as it is about having a loving attitude towards everyone. We both chose to focus on good things and keep our thoughts away from the worries. Dorka may have been the one suffering, but she was also the one who would try to tell me that everything in my life will be ok. She cared about my husband and my children, and she was giving me the encouragement to keep fighting for my marriage and family.

When she got admitted to the oncology hospital, her hopes went up, but the pain in her neck returned. She would be in pain and uncomfortable almost all the time. I made up a story that we were both climbing Mount Everest, the highest mountain in the world. This journey was even harder as we were fighting for her life.

Before Dorka got sick, she was in a long-distance relationship with a man from Belgium. She had never mentioned him to me while she was well, and I think that she never felt worthy of being truly loved.

She met her first husband when she was just 18 and lived for most of her life not honouring her values. They separated when she started voicing her needs, and she was bringing up their daughter on her own without the financial support of her ex-husband. She worked very hard in a sweet shop that she owned. She was the "I can do it all myself" person.

Even while she was dying and paralysed, she did not want to bother others. Her boyfriend called her a few times but never came to visit her, and she never commented on it. She held all her hurts inside, trying to battle them on her own. I read somewhere that those who suffer from cancer are often a victim of facing life on their own, not asking for support and not feeling worthy of that support. I have learned a lot from being present with my sister during that challenging time.

The most important lesson was that our time here is the most precious commodity. Time should never be taken for granted. We are never promised a tomorrow. Every moment that we are offered, we can just live through it without realising its significance, or we can be present and be appreciative as it was the best and only treasure to focus on. As the saying goes, "We do not know the value of something until it is gone." Very true.

I was privileged enough to be a part of my sister's journey. I have watched her every struggle, I have watched her having trouble breathing, I have heard her words, saying, "I want to live, even if I must live being paralysed. I just want to watch my daughter grow."

We all have the gift of being here for our loved ones, loving them, to be around them. Yet, so often, we waste that gift of time by worrying and complaining about them or our life. I hope that I have learned to be appreciative enough to honour my sister's journey, and that I spend every moment enjoying it as though it was the last.

Learning the True Meaning of Life

The predictions about my sister's recovery were very slim. I was often told by different doctors that there was not much hope.

I chose to silence those thoughts that would have me face losing her while she was still next to me. I would not tell my mum about those conversations that I had with the doctors. She was clinging to the hope of a miracle recovery for her daughter. I had not the heart to tell her how dire my sister's situation was.

While she spent a week at her new hospital, she was being prepared for radiation. The day before the radiation was going to commence, she got a chest infection and was transferred to ICU – the next blow on our journey. A big one. Again, she was heartbroken and heard the news from the doctors that there will be nothing more that they can do for her. I followed her bed while it was wheeled out from the room where she had made some friends and was clinging to her last hope of having a chance of survival, her last chance to live.

We get so worried about many things in life that have very little significance in the bigger picture. We get upset when someone does not like us, and we waste precious time proving to others that we are good people. We do not realise then that it is not about who we are and what we did that causes others to reject or criticise us. It is them not wanting to have someone in their presence that they are not equipped to deal with.

There is a good question that I have learned from my mentor. If something does not go the way we like it, and we choose to think that we are in a terrible situation, he would ask, "Terrible, compared to what?"

That question has helped me many times when I would feel hard done by someone. After reflection, I would realise that in the hierarchy of what is truly important to me, that challenge was way down the list and not worth the scale of stress and attention I was giving it.

The journey I have taken beside my sister has been one of the best if not the best experiences, in my life. I could see how much strength I had. I learned how much strength she had and how much love she had for everyone around her while facing the biggest battle anyone can face.

After being taken to the intensive care unit, Dorka was given extra oxygen. A small mask was placed on her face to help her breathe. I was told that there was not enough oxygen getting to her lungs, which was putting her life in danger. I was terrified that she may pass away that night. I begged the doctors to let me stay with her for the night and was told that it was not possible because it is an ICU unit. I kept talking to every doctor that I could, and they let me stay. I was given a small chair to sit next to her bed. She was relieved that I was there with her. She was very scared and heartbroken.

Her oxygen levels continued to drop during the night, and the nurse would keep adjusting her mask and check on her. Dorka kept crying and telling me that she does not like the mask on her face, that it makes her claustrophobic, and she kept moving her head and the mask would fall off.

I spent the whole night putting it back on, as the nurse told me that she would not survive without it. There were moments when I would try to keep it on her face and she would cry, move her face from side to side and try to have it off. I would get angry at her, telling her that she needs it.

It felt awful to fight with her like that. I could not imagine how horrible she felt. She was paralysed, totally hopeless and not able to take a proper breath.

The Fight for Breath

Those moments teach you what life is about. In those moments without realising it at the time, we are being carried by some extra powers, unknown to us, when things go well in life. Some call it God, Holy Spirit, some believe that those strengths and powers are always with us, we are just unaware of it.

I was very aware of that power at those times. I was learning fast that we are not just made of the matter and the spirit.

We are made with a capacity to love that gives us an amazing strength when faced with the possibility of fighting for our loved one's life.

There is this invisible line between us and the powerful universe, and when needed, we can access the energy that keeps our universe going. I got to experience it and know that, when we are calm, grateful, humble and know what we want, it is available to us.

The universe keeps recreating itself, and so do we. We have the capacity to create what we want. We are the creators of our life. The desires keep arising in us, and from those desires we move forward to fulfil them.

The process of creating what we perceive as "missing" is what the journey in life is all about. Those creations give us an array of emotions, and it is those emotions that we are after. Those moments of fulfilment where we have previously only seen a void.

The desires in us never die, because the creation of the universe must continue, and it continues through us and our desires. We may not like it when we see that something is missing in our day-to-day lives, but we are designed that way; we cannot create unless there is a contrast of having against not having. The wanted and the unwanted gets us moving in the direction of having the wanted or moving away from the unwanted. We focus on those and act in a way that gives us the possibility of having what we focus on.

I became aware that we have the power and the strength to have anything that we desire. For that lesson, I am forever grateful.

One Man's Unconditional Love that Held Me Up

During my stay in Poland, I felt very guilty that while my sister was dying, I was still heartbroken that my husband stopped loving me.

Every morning I would wake up and realise that my situation has not changed, and I had no messages from him. The anxiety would start again, but the duty to be there for my sister would take over and I would feel better by the end of the day. Nevertheless, I would go to sleep thinking about him again.

From talking to children almost every day I knew that he had moved on and was not thinking about me at all. I was, in a way, angry with myself because I was not able to get over him and feel normal again.

God has been trying to help me by sending me someone who became like an angel during my stay in Poland.

Two months after arriving in Poland, I got in touch with Krzysiek, my first love from my early teenage years. I found him on Facebook and learned he now lived in London. He knew my sister well and was saddened to hear about her illness.

Interestingly, he was just getting out of a long-term relationship. We called each other often and he became my number one supporter and the only person I could openly talk to about how Dorka's illness was progressing and how I was coping with it. I was not sharing all the details the doctors told me with Mum or my sister. They both knew that she was not in a good way, and I wanted to spare them the sad details.

With Krzysiek, I was able to be open and break down and cry when I needed to. We were both happy about reconnecting and helping each other while we were both going through relationship breakups.

It was a great distraction to talk about times when we were dating and learning about life. What I always loved about him, apart from other things, was that he made me laugh, and he always cared about me a lot. I broke his heart when we were dating. He proclaimed his love to me before joining the army, but I told him that I did not want to be with him. I cried that whole night after we parted ways. I did love him but wanted my freedom as well. I was 18 years old then.

The Pain that Only Love can Conquer

After spending the night in ICU with my sister, I left her alone during that day to get some rest. When I returned, she had tubes coming out of her mouth and she was unconscious, and I thought that it was it, that I would never look into her eyes or hear her voice again.

She did pull through. She was fighting. On the third day in ICU, the decision was made to insert the tube through her neck to be able to hook her up to oxygen. She was told that a tube would be inserted through her nose as well to feed her. She cried like a child and kept screaming, "Don't, please don't do it to me."

I was there while it was done and tears were streaming down her face. There was nothing that I could do to help. Absolutely nothing. Straight after, I would sit next to her and hold her hand. She could not feel the touch of my hand, but she knew that I was sharing every bit of her pain. Since that day she was not able to talk. Just a whisper would come out when she wanted to communicate. I learned to understand most of what she would try to say.

The most amazing thing was that when our mum, my older sister, her daughter or other family members will come to visit, while she was just lying there, unable to move or talk, she would smile at everyone. She would try to show us that she was keeping strong and did not want anyone to be upset.

Putting those words on paper and reliving those moments makes my heart sink, but at the same time, I can feel how deep and profound her love was. There she was, staring the death in the face, and she would find the strength to not make it about herself. And there I was, crying about how hurt I was because my husband chose not to love me. Such irony. And the truth was, I was still feeling the pain of his abandonment, even in those moments.

Now I know that my mind was full of lies that I chose to believe. Lies that I have created and did not want to let go of. Unfortunately, at that time and for another year after, I did not know that.

There was nothing else that could be done for my sister. She got sent to a hospice where she would wait to die. The ambulance that took her there drove off with the sirens on.

The place where she went was very depressing. A drab, old building as a part of an army hospital. The building next-door was a morgue. There were only people in their 70s, 80s and 90s there. All of them were so heavily medicated that they slept all the time. My sister was put in a room with three other elderly ladies, who were not responsive most of the time. Unfortunately, the doctors were not very nice either.

Once, a male doctor asked me to leave when he was going to examine her and see how she was going. I asked to be able to stay during the examination to be able to speak for her, as not everyone could understand her whisper. He asked me out of the room. After he was finished, she told me that he said to her that she does not need special care because she is going to die soon anyway. I could not allow for that – no one deserves treatment like that during their final days.

My baby sister was dying. She knew it, we all knew it. She was scared. Myself, my mum and my sister were just hanging in there, but I was not going to leave her to die in that place.

Again, I would beg to be able to stay the night with her when it seemed like we were going to lose her. She would say to me that she was afraid to close her eyes and go to sleep, because she worried that she would not wake up.

During the whole night, Krzysiek would keep me company by texting with me. He was saving me from losing it while I was trying to save my sister. He would write about how much he cared about me and the love he has always had for me.

It felt so amazing to be told that I am loved. My love for him was also there. I felt like the same girl who wanted to love him twenty years ago. The warm feeling that enters our hearts when we talk intimately with someone is like nothing else. The love we had for each other at that time has helped me more than I realised at the time. It was like being in a different place, far away from the hospital rooms.

I love loving and will advocate for everyone to allow themselves to want to love forever. The kind of love that is not afraid, the kind of love that does not think "what if?"

The kind of love that just wants to love. There is nothing more beautiful in this world than that feeling, the exchange of loving thoughts, words, texts and imagining being with that person.

The Last Day with My Sister

We organised for Dorka to be transported to the town where my older sister Ania lived. It was the town where my dad was buried, where all our family lived nearby – a place that was connected to our childhoods and felt like home.

The director of the current hospital made it difficult for us to transfer her, but we succeeded. For her last trip in the ambulance, I arranged to travel with her.

What was interesting was that I took the same trip with my dad when he died. I was the only one who sat in the van that was transporting my dead dad, from Krakow to Miechów. This time I was taking that trip with my sister, who was still alive, but slowly losing her battle for life.

The hospice in Miechów was wonderful. Run by nuns, with warm small rooms and great doctors. The doctor was even organising for her to have a normal bath. For all those months, she was being washed in the bed, and myself and Ania would wash her hair while in the bed as well.

During the second day there, she said that she needed more oxygen, and that she could not breathe. She started to drift in and out of consciousness.

That day I was planning to go back to Krakow for a night. A month before, Krzysiek had booked a trip from London and was going to meet me in a hotel that I rented for us. I did not know what to do. My sister was dying in a front of me, and he was flying in on the same day, coming from another country to see me. I asked Dorka what I should do. She said that she knows that he loves me very much and that I should go, and that she would be alright.

She was dying and was not worrying about herself. Even in those moments of drifting in and out of consciousness, she was thinking about what I needed. Of course she needed me there, I was by her side all the time.

I told my mum and sister Ania that I would travel to Krakow and they both could not believe that I would leave my dying sister.

I was listening to my heart and my intuition. With a heavy heart, I said goodbye to Dorka. She smiled and said that she loved me. I told her how much I loved her and thanked her for being ok with me leaving her.

That day, while she started making her way to the other side, and I had to face the thought that I was seeing her for the last time, God sent me Krzysiek, who had unconditional love for me. He was there to hold me up with the wings of his love.

Pleasure and Pain Go Together

The evening and night with Krzysiek were like no other. It was great to see him and feel wanted, loved and adored.

He was the only man in my life at that point that I knew meant every word that he said. He was my best friend, and I was very grateful for that, more than I was ever able to express to him.

My headspace was overwhelmed with worries about my sister. I kept contacting Ania to see how Dorka was doing. She fell asleep and appeared to be unconscious shortly after I left.

Krzysiek was wonderful. He had been looking forward to that romantic weekend with me for weeks. None of us could have predicted that my sister would get worse at that exact weekend. We had a lovely dinner and spent a great night together. The hotel room was rented for two nights, but the following morning I decided that I wanted to be back by my sister's side.

She did not regain consciousness, and I was only able to sit by her side and watch her sleep peacefully. After spending the day with her, my mum and sister took over at 7 PM.

The next morning, at 6am, I got a phone call from Ania that Dorka had passed away. It was the 1st of July, one month before her 45th birthday.

Mum told me that while she was with her during her last night, she kept saying to Dorka to open her eyes. She kept repeating it to her, hoping that my sister could hear her. Around midnight she opened her eyes and looked at my mum and was very peaceful.

At about 5am, Mum and Ania went to the chapel that was near the room. Dorka was being attended by the nurses then. While they were praying in the chapel, Dorka took her last breath.

Mum said that she probably did not want to take her last breath when mum and Ania were there. My sister crossed to the other side, but my love for her did not change into grief. It stayed as strong as always and grew into gratitude for being able to be by her side during the most powerful journey of life and death. Our friendship and connection were ever-present, despite not being able to enjoy each other because we lived on different sides of the world.

Now she is always in my heart, and the love for her is ever-present and fuels my life with a deep appreciation for life and a strength that can only be built from loving and being loved unconditionally.

Live Your Life Like There is No Tomorrow

My husband walked away from me when he moved out on the 11th of July the year before.

My sister passed away on the 1st of July. Two very important people have left me in the same month, in the space of one year.

I like to find significance in what life is presenting to us. What was the message for me? At that time, I was mostly numb and letting the wave of life carry me. In a way, that battle was over.

There was nothing else I could do to save my sister or have her near me.

I did not question God then. I accepted that she was at peace, that she fought as long as she could and for as long as she wanted. Deep down, I knew that she was not gone. I have felt very close to her all my life, even though we did not see each other for seven years before her illness. Our connection and love for each other were so strong and the physical distance never ruined that.

The way she faced her battle was an inspiration to me that has shaped my life since. It brought joy to my life because whenever I get caught up with feeling sorry for myself, I would remind myself how lucky I am to be alive and healthy. Then I smile at Dorka and tell her how grateful I am for her passing. She gave me the biggest gift that anyone could give me: appreciation for life as it is. Like the saying goes, "Live your life like there is not tomorrow." And then wake up tomorrow and do it all over again.

I have since learned that we experience grief because we realise we are not able to receive love from that person anymore and unable to give them our love in person. When that person is missing from our lives, there will be other people who will take on the traits that we are missing. The form will change, but the love and attention will be present, the love that we have for them is continuous. Love is shown not only through the senses but mostly felt in our hearts. That love continues and often gets stronger.

At that time, I did not know what grief was because I was exhausted after the four months of watching her struggle and battling it up with her. My trip to take mum back and return in a month had turned into becoming a full-time nurse for my little sister. When I knew that her chances of recovering were slim, I had discussions with the children, and they all agreed with me that I could not come back and leave her at that time. Later, my ex-husband made accusations through his solicitor that I had taken a holiday to Europe and was spending money. The funds that I had available went towards paying for the private rehabilitation hospital and other needs for my sister.

He cut me off our credit cards while I was in Europe as well. I was fighting two or more battles at any given time – some about the logistics of life, others in the heart. Anger, resentment, guilt and fear were constant, but I knew that it had to be a good reason for all that life had thrown at me.

Part Summary – Key Points

1. We cannot manage our finances if we cannot manage our emotions.

   We are not victims of others' actions – we are victims of our perceptions about those events.

   Everything and everyone is helping us, pushing us towards our true destiny.

2. Do not compare yourself to others - you are a gift as you are.

   Minimalizing or exaggerating yourself according to others makes you live subordinating to their values, not yours.

   Judgment of yourself or others takes your power away.

3. Nothing is ever missing from your life.

   Everything we want is always present and comes in lots of forms.

   Time is the most precious thing in life, and we all have it.

Part 5:
Love is All We Need

Love is the Answer

Everything that we are experiencing is leading us towards what we want in life. Mine was a pursuit of love, fulfilling relationships and the need to feel that I belong, and that I am connected to myself and everything around me.

During my life in Australia and my first marriage, there was always that crippling sensation that I was only living half the life that I wanted to live. It was like I had to pump myself up with the outside motivation to keep going, waiting for that *aha!* moment to hit me on the head and wake me up and let me enjoy life fully.

I never experienced that while I was living in Poland or Italy. Being in Europe, I felt that, wherever I lived or was visiting, I was at the right place at the right time. I was centred in my mind; I was joyful in my heart; and I related to the surroundings.

All the places that I have lived or visited in Australia did not feel like that. I felt out of place many times. I felt like I was talking myself into liking it. Nature lost its beauty; the people were not seeing me and I was not able to connect with them.

I kept thinking that it was the climate as I lived in the tropics, or I would say it was because I am upside down now, as Poland was on the northern side of the globe and Australia is on the south. I would blame the loss of my family and the inability to see them often because of the distance.

It was neither of those. I have always preferred warm to cold. I even used to say, "Watch out what you wish for because wishes do come true." I always wanted to be in a hot country, and I ended up in the tropics. I always wished for a hot Latino husband, and I married one.

I make friends easily, and they become like a family for me, and my real family is always with me in my heart. I believe that if we love someone, they are never away from us – they live in our hearts. I also felt loved from a distance by my parents, sisters, grandparents, cousins and aunties. I loved them all dearly as well, and those connections were ever-present with me, like invisible threads that connect us no matter the distance.

Their love for me always filled my life with the strength to achieve anything I wanted, and my love for them would keep me humble. It assured that I have what I need in life: the love in my heart for people who were close to me was all the happiness I needed to keep going.

Looking back, the idea that I was supposed to stop loving someone was something I could not bear. It is probably what caused the most anxiety in me at the time. Even while the marriage was good, I still had that everlasting emotion of something important missing. I think I was lonely because I did not know how to be 100 % honest with my husband about what I wanted from the marriage. I did not know how to ask for it, nor did I want to be bossy, and I did not know how to say no and put my foot down when I did not agree with his decisions.

My intuition told me that there were wrong decisions, and they were proven later to be so. I would state my position, but the last word belonged to my husband and his advisers – many of which were not loyal to him. We lost money and went through stressful times because my advice was not considered.

I loved my husband very much, and as much as it was frustrating that he would not listen to my advice, it did not matter that much to me, even when we lost big sums of money. I was focusing on the fact that he was doing what he wanted. I wanted him to be happy, so I let it happen.

The Universe Rewards Confidence, Not Subordination

Looking back, I know that it was not fair to myself to not honour myself and to make sure the decisions about our future were agreed together. I was diminishing myself and a subordinate to my husband's wishes, as if his wellbeing was more important than mine.

Now I know that it was my own doing. I chose that position for myself, thinking that I would be loved and appreciated more if I let him make all the decisions.

The universe does not work like that. The universe rewards us when we value ourselves enough to ask for what we want. When we minimise ourselves relative to others, we get punished because we are not recognising our worth.

The world on the outside is going to value and respect us to the degree we value and respect ourselves on the inside. As it is said in the Bible, life happens from the inside out, not the other way around.

I thought that if I was prized and recognised on the outside, then I would feel good on the inside. It does feel good, but it is not sustainable, and it does not last. By putting my husband's needs first, I was also applying the same mental state to most people around me. I usually did not know how to say no to others. My extended family, my friends and strangers would get my attention and help because I was looking for their approval. I would extend myself to help others without being asked because I felt like it is what is making me happy.

The only people I was not doing it to were my children. I think I did not fear losing their love or approval regardless of how I acted. I knew their love was and always be there. We intuitively trust our children or parents but act from a fearful place when it comes to others. For me, it was only mostly the Christian belief that I need to help others, support others and sometimes sacrifice my own desires for others.

Since then, I have learned that no one needs to be saved. Other people are all perfect just as they are, and they don't need my help unless asked, and they do not need saving. I was unhappy with life because I was unhappy with myself. I thought that if I give lots then I will get lots back. I would stupidly think that others would guess how to treat me and what I want or need to be happy. They can't. They are busy with their own life, chasing their own happiness.

So while I waited for others to notice my needs and for others to guess what I needed to be happy, I was not happy, and it was not their fault.

It was me who forgot to ask for what I wanted. My happiness was hindered because I was forgetting about myself.

I was so busy noticing everyone around me and doing what it takes to make sure they were happy and believing that because I am thinking about them, they will think about me. Some maybe did, but most did not. It was not their job to make sure that I was happy, just as it was not my job to make sure that they were happy.

It was not their fault; it was not my husband's fault. There is no one to blame for the fact that I did not get what I wanted or that I was not happy.

It is our job, and only ours, to ask for what we want or to pursue it ourselves, chasing after what makes us happy. We like seeing others being happy, and they want it for us as well. But it is a personal reasonability to take action towards it.

Loving ourselves, honouring ourselves and being true to ourselves is to ask of others for that which makes us happy, it is to look for what makes us happy and doing what makes us happy. It is our duty to ourselves and to those who care about us to take the necessary steps to have a fulfilling life.

Our happiness will give us great health and an abundance of energy to be able to share our gifts with others. Not taking care of ourselves robs others of having us fully present and contributing to the life of those we choose to love.

When we decide on the inside what a gift we are to the outside world, how worthy we are to others, then the outside world will reward us accordingly.

Facing My Fears

The confident woman that I wanted to be again started emerging shortly after starting work at the Aero Club.

I was continuing my studies with the Demartini Institute, getting personal coaching, reading and writing anytime that I could. Many diaries were piling up, and the more words that were put onto paper the clearer and lighter my head became.

I was back. Not only back to the confident, loving herself woman that arrived in Australia twenty years ago, but a much wiser one and one that was ready to face her fears. I now knew what those fears were – the fantasies that I had created in my mind, the fear that in my future some events will be more negative than positive.

Fear is a part of our journey; it is not something to try not to feel. It is there to protect us from going silly in life. It makes us stop and rethink some ideas, to make us run when we encounter danger. It is there to caution our decisions and help us see both sides to the decisions we make about our future.

That knowledge and the experience of my own life have allowed me to see that all events have always had both sides. This has become the wind to my sails. The wisdom that I acquired through exercises of finding gratitude for the hurtful events of previous years gave me the wings to fly higher than I have ever allowed myself to imagine.

The love that I felt for myself, for my husband and everyone who I have ever met, and not yet met, made me appreciate every little bit of myself and feel so connected to everyone and everything. Gratitude is felt so deeply and so profoundly, but also for a short time. It takes all our senses to be focused on the thought of appreciation without judgment. Being present in a moment and just taking time to be one with our surroundings, being humble to the divinity that created us and in awe of our own perfection – that is how gratitude felt for me.

For that, I am deeply grateful to everyone that has contributed to my growth, and especially to those who have put me through the hardest lessons of love. Those who made me cry, who have rejected me, who told me that I was not lovable, that I was not good enough for them. Those who saw me as a threat to their happiness, as a burden and an enemy. Those who were not there when I needed them, who would wish me to fall and who would close their hearts from me. They all made me realise that if it was not for their words and actions, I would have never looked at myself from the inside.

I lived life wanting to be loved, and the measure of how I was loved was how others acted around me. That is not the case anymore. I now live with the certainty that I am always loved by those around me, by those who support me, love me and those who challenge me.

"There is only love, everything else is an illusion," is a lesson I have learned from Dr John Demartini.

My journey to learn about life from this great teacher, philosopher and researcher started with my husband in 2007. At the time, it was my husband who was struggling emotionally and was unable to deal with stress and having panic attacks. We both attended many of his seminars and fell in love with his vast knowledge and wisdom.

My husband was able to overcome his anxiety and had a calmer approach to people and his business. It brought us closer as a couple. Seven years later, I was the one needing help with anxiety, and my husband has moved from being grateful for everyone to seeing me as negative energy that needs to be avoided.

I have achieved the outcome that I was looking for. My anxiety disappeared in 2015, three years on from its onset. I have not only cured my worries and anger but gained an understanding of life and learned how to love.

Feeling Worthy of Love

There was not a day that I would not write how I felt or what I wanted. The big mirror in my bathroom, all the space on my desk and my side table were covered in writing. There were pictures of the things that I wanted, there were affirmations, words of encouragement, words of hope and words of love.

I started writing long lists of wishes that I had for my future. I cut pictures from magazines and glued them to my book of wishes. There were pictures of handsome men, beautiful and confident women, luxury houses, holiday places, accessories. I had different sections: appearance, work, home, marriage, holidays. I would have multiple beautiful pictures for each section.

The little girl who would dream about her prince charming, her beautiful home, great job, sexy look, was back. I was a new person in many ways. I was looking for love, for a partner, for a new career, for a new beginning. My outlook on life changed and I knew that I wanted all those things, not because I am missing them, but because I wanted and deserved every single one of them in their purest forms.

I was not afraid to give love another chance. My heart was almost healed, and I knew that it would love not less, but with much more intensity and hunger for love.

Lots of women and men become afraid of loving again after they have been hurt, rejected or abandoned by the person they loved. I did my homework and learned that there is not such a thing as hurt, rejection or abandonment if we choose to see the full picture. Any time we perceive being rejected and abandoned by one person, others want us, support us and appreciate us.

I knew that I cannot get hurt, and I also knew that I wanted to love and be loved like crazy.

At the same time, I knew that love was not missing. I was surrounded by love, and having that knowledge made me relax, knowing that I would meet the right person when it was meant to be.

The previous year, I wanted men to be interested in me to confirm that I am worthy of love. I wanted them to notice me, to find me attractive, to want me. At that time, I was coming from a place of thinking that I would feel better if someone would love me, that it would confirm to me that I was good enough, pretty enough and so on.

The lover then appeared that played in that part of my journey. Some other men that I met mostly only for one date were just that. A plaster to my wounded womanly ego.

This time I wanted to be with someone because I was ready to have fun, to experience more, to play in the playground of relationships. I did not need a man, but I wanted one.

Creating the Life I Wanted to Live In

Ready for life and ready for love, I started telling my girlfriends that the next man in my life would be a prince on a white horse. It was my metaphor to express that I want someone extraordinary, someone who would stand out from the crowd, someone who can command respect as a prince would. Someone who would treat me like a princess.

I have grown my self-worth and knew that would not settle for anything less than someone with certain qualities. I was much calmer than the previous year when I felt lonely and impatient and I knew that my prince would appear at the right time.

At the Aero Club, there were plans for a flyover for a breakfast to Arlie Beach one Saturday morning. A few pilots were taking their planes for a spin there and back on the same day. My boss invited me to join him on his plane, and I loved the idea. Without thinking, I said that I would like to come but only if we stayed overnight.

One reason for that was that I was alone every weekend, and the idea of spending it in the beautiful town of Airlie Beach sounded wonderful. The other reason was that I was starved for company, and I liked him a lot as a boss and as a man. He was very interesting as a person and very attractive. I was not 100 per cent sure what his marital status was, but one of his friends told me once that he may be moving in with him. That for me confirmed that he was single or planning to be single.

My proposition for an overnight stay was serious, but I did not expect it to happen. I think that he was as surprised with my proposition as was I with myself saying it. Despite my apprehension, his answer was yes.

The trip over was a bit bumpy, and I was told that it was because of the many mountains we had to fly over. I was thrilled to be on the plane and next to the very capable and handsome pilot, but I was putting a brave face on and holding onto the seat with all the strength that I had.

We joined others for breakfast, and most of the planes left straight after. We were not planning to let others know that we were not returning that day, so we made an excuse to go to the town and visit the lagoon to sunbathe for a bit.

Some guys who were with us but flew on a different plane decided to join us. They were expecting us to travel back with them to the airport, and we could not hide our plans, so we told them that we were going to stay overnight and fly back the following day.

Neither of us had made any bookings for the night, and we went to the resort hotel that I liked, and we were able to get a room. The place was beautiful and one of my favourite accommodations in Arlie. It was positioned on the edge of the ocean, with a great restaurant and amazing views.

I had stayed there a few months before with one of my daughters, and at that time I was very sad and lonely. This time was different.

We had a drink in the lovely pergola next to the water, then went to the room. I was feeling a bit tired, or maybe in a bit of a shock that I was in a hotel room with a man that I liked. We both had some rest and decided to have dinner in the room. The time went quickly, and we had lots to talk about. He told me a lot about himself, and although I was not asking for it, he was very open. The evening just unfolded very easily for us as we did lots of honest talking and were not afraid of being vulnerable with each other. What followed was a beautiful night of making love and enjoying each other. I felt very relaxed and safe in his company. He was amazing with the attention he was giving to me and his willingness to give me as much pleasure as possible.

His situation was complicated, and I did not expect him to commit to me. I loved his company and was very attracted to him but knew that I did not need to force anything. I felt at peace with just living in the moment and having such a great time with him. I was amazed at how intelligent and complex he was.

I loved that he was very honest about everything and did not try to impress me. He was very confident with himself, and I liked it a lot. I love strong men who know what they want.

That was our first romantic date, and a few more followed. The children were not impressed when he would come over and stay for some weekends, but I was happy and not holding myself back from falling in love and enjoying his company.

Giving Love a Chance

I knew that there is not such a thing as getting hurt or disappointed. I knew that there are only experiences and my time on this planet is the most valuable commodity. I was not going to hold myself back from enjoying his company or his love.

The issues that my children raised when I started dating him were not concerning me that much, as I understood that they would not be welcoming anyone into their home if they had a choice. I also knew that they did not know how important it was for me – they lived in their teenage world.

I permitted myself to focus on what was important to me while being a great mother to my children at the same time. My first date with him was in March. At the end of April, I was going to Ricky Martin's concert in Townsville with one of my girlfriends. He happened to have some work to do there, so he booked a hotel and we stayed there for a few nights.

Townsville was a beautiful town to visit, and he used to live there, so he took me to see great beaches and visit the places he loved. Before that trip, I asked my son for his thoughts if my new boyfriend moved in with us. He was the youngest and spent the most time at home with me, while his sisters kept with each other. He was also my biggest supporter during my tough times. He looked after me, helped around the house, the garden and was my man in the house. His approval was important to me. So far it was a "no."

When we came back from that trip, my son wanted me to buy a skateboard for his best friend's birthday. It was quite a costly one, and I was not agreeing with the idea. His friend wanted to use it to get to school, and I was worried that he might injure himself on it because it was a big skateboard. When we were walking out of the shops, my son had tears in his eyes. He cared about his friend. He then said that if I buy that skateboard as a gift for his friend, then he will be ok with my new boyfriend moving in. To this day it is a fun story for us as my son probably contributed to Gary being my husband now.

It was only two months from our first date when he moved in, but at that stage in my life, I was not interested in slow dating and not being able to get to know someone on all levels. I knew that as easy as relationships start, they can end. There are no golden rules to follow.

When I was with my first husband, we dated for three years, married for fifteen, had a great relationship and it ended just like that. My sister was super healthy for 44 years, then she collapsed and was dead in five months.

I was not going to waste time on deciding what is good and what is not, dwelling on if it was the right choice or not; I choose to listen to my heart and follow my intuition. It was always right if I listened.

That year, I and Gary opened a restaurant together and got engaged. The engagement was also my idea. I told Gary that I am not girlfriend material. It was not about the piece of paper, it was about me respecting myself and wanting to be called a wife, not a partner, as well as knowing that if it was not important to him but important to me, if I mattered as much as I wanted to, then he will want to be my husband.

I asked my children to tell their dad that he should get the divorce papers ready, as he was the one who chose to leave the relationship first. A friend brought the divorce papers to our restaurant. The date was the 20 of August 2015. On that exact date two years before the first solicitor letter arrived. It was the date we got married 15 years ago.

The Promise of Love and Marriage

We planned a trip to Arlie Beach, where we had our first date. The weather is always beautiful there and the place is magical.

There was a night of the full moon and we went to the beach. I kept asking Gary to take photos of me and the moon, and he told me later that he wanted to propose to me in that spot, but I ruined the moment by asking for the photos. He did propose that night, just in a different spot on the beach. I said yes.

The following year we opened the second restaurant. We worked hard and survived the many storms that come with opening new businesses and working together. We had three teenagers at home and lots of issues that were still a part of my last relationship. I knew that if we survived through it all, then we would make it as a couple.

It was not easy; we worked every day from early morning till late at night as both restaurants were part of the hotels. We were operating from 6 AM for breakfast, till the last guests left at night-time. We ran room service as well. We were very proud of what we have achieved. We met lots of great people and had many wonderful moments enjoying time with our customers and friends at our venues.

We chose to have our wedding near the beach at the beautiful golf course that was part of the Halliday Bay Resort in August. My first wedding was on Hayman Island, in a chapel on the top of the mountain. This one was just metres from the ocean and in the open, surrounded by palm trees.

The setting was breath-taking and the weather picture perfect. I was a bit worried that the evening may be too cold, as our dinner party had an open setting. I was very pleasantly surprised when the sun went down and there was not a breeze, the evening was warm. The moon that appeared was a beautiful surprise.

All the people that were important to me were there, unlike the first one when I was not able to have anyone from my family. My mum and sister came over from Europe, my girls were my bridesmaids and my son walked me to give me away to Gary and was a groomsman along with Gary's long-time friend, David. My beautiful friend Viviana, who I'd known since my children were small, was there as my Maid of Honour.

A month before the ceremony, one of the pilots from the area offered to fly me to the ceremony in his private helicopter. I even had a choice of a yellow or a blue one! Only I, Gary, the owner of the resort and a close friend knew that I was going to arrive at the reception from the sky. The bridesmaids arrived in golf buggies and everyone was waiting for me to arrive in a buggy as well. I arrived in a blue helicopter and loved every moment of it.

I have found my prince on the white horse, but he was a modern prince, and instead of a horse, he had a white plane. That day, I married my prince, the sun was shining, the birds were singing, the day was magical, like from a dream. That day I married a man who become my husband and my best friend. A friend who has helped me restore my faith in myself.

He has become my mirror who tells me every day about how beautiful and perfect I am, as well as that there is still much more that I can achieve.

Messenger of Love

I believe that in life nothing is a coincidence, that there is some order to where we find ourselves and who we encounter on our journey.

My first husband's name translates to *Messenger,* and he was in my life to love me and wake up the love in me. He has succeeded. He was in my life for the length of time for me to learn what I needed to learn. He has given me everything that I wanted as a wife and mother. When there was no more that I could learn, he was the messenger who has delivered the news that I did not like but needed to hear to be able to experience what I always wanted to experience. He was the messenger who redirected my life so I could go, look for and find all the answers that I needed and wanted to find. He has put me onto the road where I found my new husband. Thanks to his actions, I was able to meet someone who has become my soul mate, my best friend, my lover, my everything in life.

The lessons that I have learned on my journey of self-discovery meant I was able to love unconditionally and know that I was loved without questioning it. To make things interesting, there are few similarities when it comes to both men.

While living in Italy, I learned to speak German and Italian – both of those languages were needed to work there. I was better at German but liked Italian more. My first husband was born in Australia, but both his parents were Italian. We spoke Italian when we would visit his parents and family. My second husband is Austrian, and I speak German with his parents.

I met the first one in the town of Bolzano in Italy, the second one's family comes from a town half an hour from Bolzano, called Merano. I even visited the town while I lived in Italy. Both towns are surrounded by the beautiful Dolomite Mountain Range.

While living in Italy and dating my first husband, for his birthday I bought him a local cookbook in Italian. In that book, I wrote a dedication in four languages: Polish, English, Italian and German.

When my second husband moved in, among his possessions was the same book. The same cover, the same content, but written in German. The universe truly works in mysterious ways.

One more similarity was that I and Gary have lost our dads suddenly and tragically. We were both living in foreign countries when they died. My dad's aorta burst, killing him when no one was around. Gary's dad's apartment caught on fire while he was alone, and he died while trying to climb down the balcony. They both died on the same day: the seventh of December.

We said to each other that our dads have helped us find each other. We both feel blessed that we found each other, both being far away from our homelands. My wish always was to feel comfortable with the people around me.

I love sharing my love towards others and want everyone to feel good around me, and I was hoping to be able to learn how to feel good around others. I have achieved that. In Gary, I found that special someone who makes me feel good about myself, who makes me feel wanted, needed, appreciated and loved more than I know how to love myself.

He has made me the queen of his castle and offered himself to me with trust and love similar to that of a child towards its mother. He has made me a part of himself, and in return, I have made him a part of me.

Those special connections that poems and songs are written about do exist. There are not visible from the outside as they are not physical in nature. They are felt at specific moments and only understood by those who made the choice and commitment to silence the fears and let the heart do its work.

My everyday life is a fairy tale. Not one that is fragile and in danger of disappearing at midnight. A fairy tale that I write and live every day. My soul is the guide that creates the script. My mind is the director that approves of it with trust. My body is the vessel that acts it out so I can indulge all my senses in experiencing the joys of life.

The Essence of Life is Love

The essence of life is love.

Love drives us to keep going in life. The love for nature gives us hope and healing. The love for others gives us courage. The love for ourselves gives us a reason to indulge in life's pleasures.

Choosing love gave me the strength to keep going. The knowing that when I slip down with doubt and worry, I can choose love over and over and get myself back onto the road forward. We all do not know where we are going – some of us even do not know why we keep getting ourselves up and keep pushing forward. No one answer would satisfy everyone when it comes to the big questions about love and life.

Love gives life and love makes us want to end life. Love gives wings and knocks us down with the heaviness of hurt from love. Love saves us from suffering and is the reason for suffering. Love is responsible for the most beautiful art and music being created and is responsible for life being lost. Loves make us a better people and can also turn us into villains. Love is something we dream of and is what some are afraid of.

That is my proof that everyone and everything in life can be a builder and a destroyer at the same time. The giver and the taker. The amazingness and the ugliness. The reason to live, the reason to die.

On my journey in life, I have encountered many people. Australia is the third country that I call home. I remarried. I reinvented myself. I started new friendships. Many choices were my own decisions, some choices were made from the necessities to keep going forward.

Whatever drives us in life, whoever we encounter, whatever turn we take, there is no reason to look back and wonder what could have been if we did take a different turn. All roads lead to the same destination, and while none of us knows what and where it is, it still is the same destination. The aim is to be aware that there is no need to overthink that journey.

We often look to the sides and compare our lives to those around us. We keep thinking that we could have what others have or be like others. It is good to be inspired by someone and chose to learn and achieve what we perceive as an improvement, but it can be destructive if we start feeling less fulfilled thinking that others may have it better.

Everyone is fighting their battles, and what may look from the outside like a happy life, may not be as happy if we knew what was going on inside of others or inside of their families.

Everyone is faced with challenges to make us grow. Everyone is equipped to tackle them. Some will fold as I did from the start; some will be stronger than others. There is no right or wrong way to face those challenges. I have learned not to judge what was a right move and what was not. There were times when I was very angry with myself for losing it and responding with anger towards my husband, my children and my mum. I thought that I could do things better, be better at controlling my emotions.

I had to decide that there is no such thing as doing something better. Being me and acting how I did at the time is the only thing I could do, and not feeling guilty about it was something I had to learn. The practice of finding benefits for others and myself when I perceive that there are only negatives was my saviour.

In the same way, I looked for benefits to see that other actions towards me were not only hurtful to me but also beneficial. When I have acted in a way unappreciated by others, I would find benefits to them and myself, and the guilt and shame would dissolve.

An Hour of Wisdom with Dr John Demartini

During my meeting with John Demartini, I mentioned my concerns that I have been very up and down around my children, that they have seen me being depressed, angry, crying, shouting, swearing at my ex and manic at times when I would try to practice gratitude and say that everything is fine.

During my early sessions with counsellors, I was told to not cry in front of the children and do it with my friends instead. I was not as open with my friends, but I was able to be 100 % myself with the children. Dr Demartini said that we should not try to pretend that we are ok if we are not. His exact words were that I could end up with cancer if I tried to bottle up my feelings.

Another important point of view he shared with me was that by being honest with myself and my children about how I feel and acting it out, I permit them to live a life that is real and shows them that whatever we do or don't do, we are worthy of love.

I had the same worries about inviting my friend Krzysiek from England to come and stay with me. I felt that I was too messed up emotionally, financially, and even physically to be able to have someone around me. His advice, again, was that it is the best time to start new closer relationships. The reason for that is that when we are vulnerable and fragile, when our lives are out of order, others can be more comfortable around us, knowing that if they are ever to lose it, we will understand, because we have been there ourselves.

That was a very significant piece of advice. I was told that we do not need to have it all together, as we are usually told, to still be a great parent, partner, or friend. He said that it is more beneficial for us because those who still choose to be around us are accepting us for the whole that we are. They also learn that they can act out and be loved as they are.

That is also how teenagers learn that there is nothing wrong with them. They act out, slam doors, tell their parents that they hate them and don't apologise for being who they are. And they are meant to do that. That way they learn to be true to who they are and how they feel. It prepares them for their relationships. When they act out with their parents and are still told that they are loved unconditionally, they learn that they can be themselves with their future partners, and still be loved and accepted.

The children that are shouted down and not able to be rebellious and act out their frustrations often grow up not knowing how to speak up for themselves. They suppress their true feelings and bottle things inside. That creates relationships that are dishonest and one-sided. That person may try not to be a trouble, try not to upset their other part and end up being unfulfilled in a working or intimate relationship.

Choosing a “Caring” Relationship

There are three types of relationships: the caring one, the careful one and the careless one.

In life and relationships, everyone is faithful to their values, not to their partners. We find a partner that fulfils those values that are at the top of our hierarchy list. People move on from relationships when one or more of those top values are not fulfilled anymore.

The key to good relationships is knowing the values our partners hold and to act in a way so that those can be fulfilled. As important as knowing and respecting their values is, knowing our own and making sure they are validated.

In a caring relationship, both partners know each other’s values and act in a way that accommodates them both. In a careful relationship, one of the partners knows and values the needs of the other and is always careful not to upset them. The other is not caring about the values of their partner. A careless relationship is one where both parties are not interested and are careless about each other’s needs, only focusing on themselves.

Some people will stay in a relationship even when they are not respected as they wish because their top values are the children and their wellbeing, or their social status, religious beliefs, or financial fears.

I came to believe that was how my younger sister got sick and passed away. She was very caring towards others and wanted everyone to be happy, but never did she ask for what was important to her.

She was the youngest. The older sister was the one who mostly did the right thing and acted responsibly. I was the second and the middle one. I was loud and outspoken. When I did not agree with someone or something I would be vocal about it. Mum got to call me Histeryczka, hysterical, because I would come to screaming fights with her about how I felt. I was the one who, for the most part, did not hold stuff in.

Between me and my younger sister, there were two years of difference. So, we were all close in age, but somehow, I did much more with Ania than with Dorka. She was only 18 when she got into a serious relationship and they were travelling abroad a lot and always together. We were not able to connect at that important time because of that.

Dorka was somehow the quiet one. She was also the most beautiful one. I remember one winter evening being at my grandparent's home. It was a cold night. We were sitting close to the stove and watching the logs of wood burn – my grandparents did not have heating. Dorka was maybe six or eight years old. She had a winter beanie on, and her eyes were blue like the sky, her face was covered with freckles. I kept looking at her face and thinking how symmetrical and beautiful she was. She grew up to be taller than us, with a beautiful body and blonde, thick hair. I used to tell her when we were teenagers that I wanted her to be a model. There were always men wanting to date her.

She was shy. She was never loud or outspoken. Ania and I seemed to be doing better at school subjects, and maybe that made her feel like she had not much to say. Maybe there were the boys that would always be around her and take her away from spending quality time with me and Ania.

I believe that she did not know how beautiful inside and out she was, and because she did not used to ask for much for herself, she was trying for those around her to be happy, she lived with lots of regrets.

There was still so much music left inside of her that she could have blessed others with. She is doing it now from the above.

Saying "Yes" to All My Desires

Once I found all the answers I was looking for, I realised that they apply to all areas of life, with no exception. My first step to getting what I want in life is knowing what it is that I want.

Many people, when asked, "If you could have anything in the world, what would you ask for?" must think hard about the answer. It is not about the general, "I will ask to be happy." Being happy means different things to different people.

For me, there is usually a list for every area of my life. Now I know that we are here to experience joy, and to lack joy is the inability to ask for what we want and the knowledge that we deserve it. The Universe/ God wants to give us everything that we want. The more we ask, the more we are honouring God.

As said in the Bible: "Fear not little flock, for it is your Father's pleasure to give you the Kingdom." We are meant to ask and have faith that we will receive it.

The second step is knowing why I want it. We ask for the things that we believe will enhance our experience of life. When we know why we want something, it comes to us faster. We can imagine having it, we can imagine how having it will make us feel. That emotion of knowing how it will feel to have it is the fuel that is needed to manifest it.

The third step is to plan and see as many details of our desire as possible. I write down what I want. I try to describe and imagine it with every detail that is important to me. Like designing our dream home, we would not tell the builder to just build a house. He could build a shack. We would put in all the details that we want in our dream house.

The universe likes details. In those details is our heart and our uniqueness. It is the heart that brings the desires to our physical reality.

We are spiritual beings having a physical experience. Anyone who says that they do not need the material things in life because the spiritual ones are more important is denying the spirit being able to fully express itself.

The matter is never without spirit. Spirit is never without matter.

"Spirit without matter is expressionless. Matter without spirit is motionless. The two must be integrated if you want to master your life." That is one of my favourite quotes from Dr John Demartini.

Spirituality is not solely a part of religion. Everyone is spiritual in their pursuit of achieving what is significant to them. For some, it is to build a temple, a yoga studio, to have followers. For others, it is to bless others with the love of cooking and gather people together around the table where they share that love with one another. For yet another person, it could be to be a great mother, a great artist, a great leader of a business.

Our spirit can be and wants to be expressed in any way we chose to honour it and follow our calling in life. The physical part is the part that allows us to express ourselves. Both are equally important, and one can do not exist without the other. Denying the importance of one cancel the fulfilment of the other.

The fourth step in creating and getting what we want in life is I think the most important one. It is to do nothing. It is to let it go. It is moving on with life and allowing the Source (Universe/God) to bring it to our physical reality.

Allowing means not so much trusting that it is on its way, but rather not worrying about it. When we say we trust that something will happen the way we want, we have expectations, which can create impatience and worry. Our job is to ask and allow. It is always given; it is always on the way. Even if the way fills bumpy or too long. Allowing means being in a state of joy. Being in love with life.

We create beautiful experiences for ourselves when we are grateful, joyful, and present. We create unpleasant experiences when we are stressed for long periods, not appreciative, complaining and not happy with life. That is why the emotions of love, like and hope, feel so good. They are the signposts to keep reminding us why we are here. To love, to feel joy.

When stress kicks in, we are looking for ways to escape it. It is not a state we want to be in for long, as it feels off balance. It is our soul telling us that we are off the road on our journey to experience life. Choosing to appreciate, to love, to look for blessings in crisis takes us back onto the road that we are meant to be on.

Imagining My Future

When I was on my own, after my husband walked out on our marriage, I would write in different journals about what it was that I wanted. For almost three years, it was for him to come back. When I would write it, I felt pain and was reinforcing the sense of being rejected and lonely. From that place, I was creating more pain for myself.

All those years, as my hopes faded away, I would cut out pictures of magazines and imagine how I wanted my life to be. They were a few sections, as I needed and wanted change and improvement in almost all areas of my life.

There was beauty. I would glue pictures of beautiful models to a page. Their faces were not only beautiful but had a radiant smile, and they wore the clothes I wanted to see myself in.

There were houses. Pictures of kitchens, living rooms, gardens that represented the happy, comfortable home that I wanted.

There were vacations. Pictures of happy families on an island, in Europe, in nature. My wish was to be able to have those times again with my children.

There was vocation. Pictures of models dressed very elegantly and professionally with laptops, in the office, getting into expansive cars. I wanted to be them, to be able to dress like them, to feel confident, to have a job, to be someone.

There was marriage and love. Pictures of couples on their wedding day, hugging, looking happy and in love. Pictures of beautiful weddings and honeymoon destinations.

In the absence of those in my life, creating those journals was like being those models, being in those places, having that someone special next to me and creating memories with the children. The power of imagination and visualisation is the most powerful creative force.

I advise everyone to write down their dreams and goals, as well as to have visual boards. I constantly surround myself with pictures of everything that I wish to have or experience in life. I did not open that journal that I created in 2014 until 2019. My life was going at a very fast rate from 2015, with a new man, a new job, new businesses, new adventures. I was living everything that I wished for.

It was interesting to open one journal and find a picture of a beautiful blonde model standing next to a handsome pilot who was helping her up onto a small, private plane.

At the time of putting it there, I did not focus on the plane; it was about the model that I liked. Her beauty, her owning the world, her commanding respect was what made me choose that picture. I have since met my handsome pilot with a plane. I was being taken to many different beautiful destinations.

I had a picture of people enjoying themselves in a restaurant that I had attached to a sign saying, "Sorry, out living the dream, be back soon." It was a hanging sign that I got for my birthday. At the time, I was hoping to maybe take the restaurant over from my ex while we were trying to divide our assets. The year after, I opened two restaurants with my partner Gary.

I married Gary in a beautiful coastal location, and with him I travelled to Europe, visiting some amazing places in Austria, Liechtenstein, Germany, Italy and Poland.

I wore beautiful clothes, felt like a model and was a princess to my prince. All those pictures created the life I wanted to live in my imagination. They all become what I lived, and so much more.

The New Me

I have become a new person in a process of reshaping my thinking, especially in changing my beliefs. I have learned to act differently when I come across an event where I feel like I am being mistreated, misunderstood or ignored.

The emotion of hurt arises as it used to before, but my reaction to it has changed. I would recognise it and try to not react to it for as long as I can. Then, I will choose to act on it.

The acting instead of reacting made all the difference. That change made it possible for me to be a very different wife from the one I used to be. The thoughts of wanting to change my new husband to be happier are rarely there. The acceptance of him as he is made all the difference and has saved us many times from major marital dramas. "If we love people for who we are, they become the people we love". It works.

My relationship with Gary is the dream relationship I always wanted. These kinds of relationships are created from a place of wanting to accept each other, from helping each other, from seeing the big picture when things get tough. He is the prince of my first dreams about a partner and husband for life. He not only shows his love through his actions but by accepting me for everything that I am. I can see the love he has for me in his eyes when he looks at me, can feel it from him when he is close to me and sense it even when he is not next to me.

The level of intimacy we created is something that only we both can understand, and it is always felt on a very deep level when we are together. A simple touch, hug, kiss or just looking at each other speaks volumes for us because we know that it is full of love and adoration for each other. He has made it his life purpose to make me happy. I love nothing more than when I can see him relaxed, connected to me and certain of my loyalty, admiration and love for him.

It feels like having a guardian angel in my life. It feels like being home wherever I am. It feels like heaven on Earth when I think about him and the experiences we create. He often says that he can't handle seeing me unhappy and that I am the most beautiful woman in the world for him – the whole package, as he puts it.

I know it is something that does not come from luck or from wishful thinking. I believe we both put lots of work for our relationship to work and flourish the way it does. For me, it was the change from wanting my husband to be the way I would love him to be to loving him the way he is and appreciating him being as he is. Dreams are first created in our imagination, then if we are not abandoning them, life will put us on the road to having them come true.

When we stay true to ourselves and keep being like a child who believes that if we are good, Santa will bring us the presents we want, we get what we want.

Being in the state of appreciation, gratitude, enthusiasm and excitement is the road to have that what we wish for. I have learned to look for things that bring me joy in all aspects of life. Having a cup of tea, thinking about a beautiful memory, calling a friend, listening to my favourite music, looking at the nature around me. All those little things make a big difference in helping to redirect our thoughts.

Mother's Love

My three children were one of the reasons to put those words on paper. To go back to some of the hardest times and acknowledge that I have been down, in very dark places, that it all happened and that it was the hardest battle I had to fight. Only people who felt fear taking over every fibre of their being and sucking the life out know what I am talking about.

I do not want to forget those times because remembering makes me determined to make the most of the times when I am whole again. I am not free of fear, but now I see it clearly when it approaches and know how to face it with different weapons compared to the ones I tried to fight it with off the first time around.

My new magic weapon is noticing my perceptions of not liking or fearing something and working on those perceptions before they reinforce themselves as fear. I no longer try to avoid challenges now; I do not move away from people or tasks that feel uncomfortable. I try to be very slow to judge something good or bad. I would like my legacy to be a trace of not only the love I have expressed towards others, but also the big lessons that have come my way, reshaped me, and the hope that I am able to pass them on to others.

My children at the time were the reasons I kept the faith to not only beat the depressive state but to find the cause and the cure. The love I had and have for them kept me alive and gave me the strength to keep going. They believed in me when I did not believe that I was worthy of love or strong enough to overcome my emotional battles and be normal again.

Each of them presented me with their unique strengths and characteristics that were pure as gold and poured love into the wounds of my heart. They were there to dry my tears, to listen to my complaints, to pick up the pieces of me and put me back together when the pain was breaking me apart.

I become very close with them because there was not a part of me that they did not see, not a bit of me that they have not witnessed on display. Everything from screaming in anger through to praying together, to feeling love and gratitude. They have become very strong individuals because they had to deal with the challenges of the storm that is separation and the divorce of their parents.

They hated what was happening at the time and the role they had to play in being the protector to each of the parents, as well as trying to be good children to each of them.

At the same time, they all were trying to survive the most difficult teenage years and high school. My son was nine, the girls eleven and thirteen when it started, then it continued till they all finished high school. Somehow, they held it together through it all and came out the other side of that storm as very balanced and strong emotionally individuals. They all know what they want, speak their mind and have great dreams for their future.

I believe that what they have witnessed and experienced has given them an early insight into what true relationships are like and how being true to yourself, looking for positives in everything and choosing to love no matter what brings balance to life.

They have witnessed many of my lows when I was being a victim as well as all the steps of my journey to transform into the confident and loving life woman I am today.

Loving All of Me

A true relationship with others is possible if we have a true and honest relationship with ourselves. Such a relationship is possible if we learn to accept our past, our actions and have no regrets. When we are not looking back and wishing that we had acted differently, we have accepted that we lived with honesty. We understood that there was nothing to be ashamed of or change. We see our perfection in every action regardless of how others want to judge it.

Being honest with ourselves is not wanting to hide any part of us. It is to celebrate us when we have a down day and others are annoyed or angry with us, as well as when we are super happy and annoy others with all the joy that we want to share.

That honesty was on display for my children from the onset of my marriage breakdown. Before that, they had a caring, loving mum. A mum that was always there to support them, take care of every need they had. The mum who would cry in her bedroom when she was sad so they would not get upset. The mum who would try not to raise her voice during the arguments with their dad to avoid scaring them. The mum who would carry on even while she was not well and would not ask for help.

That mum considered herself a good mum. She *was* a good mum and a good wife, just not an honest one. Not one that was accepting herself. She believed the lie that in order to be loved we need to live a life trying not to upset others.

The marriage troubles allowed me to take those masks off, to be the raw me. The me that I did not like to start with while I was still clinging to the belief of a one-sided world. At the same time, it was the new me that did not care what the children thought of me, as there was not enough strength for that. That raw me just wanted to survive another day with as little anxiety as possible.

We can only give others true gifts if they are coming from a pure heart. I believe that at those times I was the pure me, and the gifts they were receiving were priceless. The promise that I made to myself to never allow myself to slip into deep fear again led me to have no fear of how others see me and how they judge me. I am not here to waste my time and try to control their judgment of me. I have not the slightest bit of control over it. What I have control over is how I react to it.

Since learning that I am everything that others see in me, I no longer worry about controlling the opinions of others around me. I also know that having all the traits that I do makes me perfect. It is how I see myself now: perfect, with nothing that I would want to change about myself.

I went through a period when I was expecting my children to understand me better, to support me better, to act differently. I came to understand that the way they acted was always the right way. It was a part of me that needed to grow, a part that needed to learn gratitude for them as they are.

They continue to be a big part of my journey. They are adults now, with very strong connections and appreciation for each other. I see them as strong individuals who are not afraid of life and accept all the challenges they come across. I am forever grateful to their dad for the choices he made. Thanks to his actions, we all have learned the true meaning of relationships and life.

Sharing My Wisdom

When I was told that others may benefit from me putting my experiences onto paper and writing about the lessons I have learned, I decided to do so. I wanted to create a piece of work that would captivate the reader and the content will ring true with almost everyone.

We all have relationships, we all run into challenges and we all hurt. We are all chasing love and fulfilment. We see different roads in front of us to try and tackle life, to find what we perceive will make us happy.

Often, we make choices in a split second of excitement or anger; sometimes we take advice or think things through. I wanted my experiences to serve as a reflection that whatever action we will chose to take to achieve the wanted outcome, there are no wrong roads. They are all leading to the same destination.

The destination is called fulfilment, joy, service to others. Whatever we are set to achieve, that purpose is always right. Because it is unique, it is ours and valid at the time.

I was thinking that I need to come up with something extraordinary in some way, then I realised that my life was and is and will always be extraordinary. Every human being and every small or big creation of nature around us is extraordinary because it is unique and not replicable.

What I have learned on my journey of wanting to heal my broken heart has become my bible for life. The lessons apply to everyone I encounter and to all areas of life. The hurt that I was trying to heal were the fears that I had to overcome.

No one likes the word "fear." It makes us think of scary staff, of unwanted emotions and facing challenges that make us want to hide. My broken heart was full of fears. Fears of facing life alone, of not being worthy of love, of missing out, of my children facing struggles, of not having the means to live.

Most of the clients that I have coached for broken relationships or loss of loved ones were having fears of not being able to move forward without that person. They were missing that person in their physical form because with them came the comfort of knowing that they will be near if needed. Trying to imagine the future without them in it was painful and scary.

Love is eternal. Love is not something that can be touched or created at will. Love is a choice. Love is a thought that we appreciate and are grateful for, whether that's a person, an animal or part of nature.

When a loved one is not near us because they made that choice or have passed away, the love that we have for them is still in us. I chose to keep loving my ex-husband, wherever he is, because loving him feels great and no one can take it away from me. Not him, not anyone else. Loving someone is a choice.

I chose to keep loving my sister, wherever she is, because loving her feels great and no one can take it away from me.

I chose to try and love those who dislike me, wherever they are because loving them feels great.

I realised that when we are loved by others we cannot feel it, we can only experience it through our senses: hearing their words of love, being touched, receiving presents, having them around us. We feel their love when we choose to think about them lovingly.

When we have an admirer that proclaims to love us and showers us with presents and compliments but we are not interested, it feels like a nuisance. So, it is not the love that we are receiving from others that feels great, it is the choice of thoughts that we decide to have about someone that makes us feel what we call love.

This was the discovery of a lifetime for me – my formula for life.

I am sure that others have come to that realisation as well, but for me, it was a breakthrough. I decided to love as much as I know how to, I decided to keep redirecting my thoughts to find love and appreciation whenever I would dislike someone, was disliked or was fearful.

We can be loved by many, as I was during my depression, and are not able to see it, feel it or be saved by it. We can also choose to love, even if we think that we are not loved by many.

Choosing to love makes us see the beauty around us, makes us feel on top of the world and saves us from fearing life.

What is Life?

I see life as a road through the woods. Not an asphalt or concrete road, but a track covered with soil. It is a beaten track as many have walked before us and made a clear visible way through the forest of life.

Walking into the woods and the road being curvy, we cannot see how long it is and if it is going to be smooth or covered with rocks. We do not know if it is going to be flat, going up or down at times. We know nothing about the road in the woods that we are choosing to take.

It is my metaphor for life: the road in front of us. There is no map that we can open and check the destination we are heading towards. Sometimes we may have some ideas about places that we want to live at or visit. We may have some plans for what we want to do while on that journey. We plan and dream about who do we want to have by our side while we are travelling.

The plans, ideas, goals and dreams, are all but a thought conceived in our minds that make us feel better when we try to imagine that journey into the unknown.

We all have those goals or wishes. We all want to have an input into that journey. I am convinced that we have more power over what we experience on that road than we think we are. We create a thought first, then we act on it.

We make a meal, build an object and draw a plan. We take a trip or make a phone call. Every action starts from a thought in our mind.

Where do those thoughts come from? Some will be deliberate, like when we are hungry we will create a meal, when we are lonely we will organise to meet with someone.

What about those thoughts that are not wanted? I have experienced that when I wanted for something and did not let the thoughts of doubt enter my mind too often, those dreams became my reality. We are what we think. We get what we think about the most. We attract what we want and what we do not want equally if we give it enough thought time.

The creation is powered by strong emotions. The point of creation is our mind and heart combined, something wanted with a strong faith and conviction becomes reality because we gave it power from the depth of our hearts.

Something not wanted but given lots of fuel from the fears living in our hearts becomes a reality because the emotion we were emitting was so strong that we have brought it to us.

We are the creators of our reality. We are the guides on our life journey. We are the ones who choose the path. Deliberate thoughts give us what we focus on, the wanted and the unwanted.

Einstein said it beautifully:

"Everything is energy and that is all there is to it. Match the frequency of the reality you want and you cannot help but get that reality. It can be no other way. This is not philosophy. This is physics."

What about the thoughts that come in uninvited? The ones that create havoc, that make us upset, that create anxiety. Where do they come from and why with such a force? That question was part of my journey. It was something that I wanted the answers for, more than the ones about getting what we want in life. Those unwanted thoughts have robbed me of precious time, and I was not able to enjoy the beauty of life around me and the love that I was surrounded by. My life was full of blessings, but my mind would block them out and keep the dark ones in. Those thick, dark ones crowded my mind to the point of not being able to see enough of the beauty around me to experience joy.

The answer that I found for myself is that those unwanted thoughts were my heart and my soul crying and shouting to me to stop focusing on what I was giving most of my attention to. At the time, I was focusing on what was scaring me in my husband's behaviour. I was frightened that it would lead to ruining our connection and understanding. I was fearing losing my marriage and my family. My soul was making me anxious to try to stop me from doing what I was doing.

The strong judgment that I had in my heart about the philosophies and beliefs that I was opposed to brought on the emotions of anxiety and stress.

When I find myself in similar situations now, when I perceive something to be in opposition to my views, I put lots of effort into seeing it as an event or opinion. I do not want to be either black or white, the right one and someone else wrong. I have suffered enough having that simple outlook.

Not everyone will agree with me, and that is understandable. We can only see life in light of our lessons and conclusions. I would invite my reader to maybe just try to see the grey sometimes and to accept that maybe we are all right in our opinions.

For me, taking that approach has taken off the burden of wanting to change or improve others or the world around me. The one who has created it all, God or the Universe, has done a great job, and anytime when I try to question it, I would get a headache, pain in my body or fear emerging in my heart.

Prizing others and the surrounding brings calm, order to my mind and joy to my heart. To be able to have joyful experiences is why we are here. To see beauty in our reflection in a mirror, and in others is why we are here. Praising the creator when we look around and see the colours of the world around us is why we are here. Feeling the warmth of the sun and the coolness of the wind is why we are here. The road that we are walking on will give us all those joyful experiences.

We do not have to worry about whether it will be up or down, straight or curved, through thick bushes or open space. All we must do is to choose to love what we encounter.

Finding Myself Inside My Heart

In one of my diaries written in 2005, I wrote about how I felt when I was living at home with a dad who drank too much, the challenges that I was facing and how hopeless I felt.

"There was once a girl who loved life. She loved almost everything that surrounded her, but it was the peace that she loved the most. Peace in her heart. When she did not have to fear the unknown. When she was not sad, awaiting pain. Pain in the heart that she knew would come.

She used to always wonder, how is it possible that the people around her can laugh, enjoy life, plan their lives during those days, when she was in a state of fear, awaiting pain. She felt sorry for herself because there was no one who could save her, no one who could give her hope so that one day she would not have to be afraid. She was hoping for a day when she did not have to feel ashamed in front of others.

Why? That question was coming back over and over. But there was no one to ask. Why did it have to be that way? She wanted to find someone who would be able to give her the answer. 25 years is a very long time –it amounts to 9125 days of fear, pain, feeling sorry and ashamed. That is 9125 days when this girl and the then-young woman has not heard that she is pretty, smart, good or just the same as others, just normal.

She had her faith, her God, saints and angels. They were always there, never abandoning, always listening, and they understood without words being spoken. They were her hope.

They believed in her and knew that this girl was somehow special and had something to offer others. It is thanks to those angels that she has survived. She trusted in them, she prayed to them, and they have always helped. She will never forget that moment when she was standing on the balcony. She was scared when she was on that balcony, because so often, on those sad days, those days without much hope, it was talking to her. It was saying, "You can jump down. You will become an angel when you die young."

There was a beautiful view from that balcony, A view onto her world, the world she wanted to love so much. A view of the sky, trees, flowers, birds, people."

That little girl who started writing her first pages in her diaries was back. That girl was asking what this world is all about and why she feels like she does not fit in. This time she has found her place in the world. She had answers to her questions. She found herself inside her own heart.

She had been there all along but was too busy worrying about everyone around her, and she was not able to hear that tiny voice calling from inside.

At those times, she thought that she was not important enough to put herself at the forefront and focus on what was important to her. She had done it before, so she did know how to do it, she just chose not to. Her want to be loved and accepted when she entered a new country and a marriage blinded her, and she forgot about herself.

But it is still there, in her own heart, that she chose to live surrounded by the love from her own beating heart.

That is what I wish for you.

Do not give up until you find yourself back in the comfort of your own heart. In that place that feels like you belong. You have created the wish to be here, as you are, creating from love, creating love with every beat of your heart.

Saved by Love

I was lucky to stumble upon a knowledge that took me from a depth of despair and has transformed my past traumas and future fears into unconditional love, gratitude and secured the enjoyment of life.

Knowledge itself was not enough to free me from my dark thoughts and uncertain future. It was the decision to apply that knowledge, to train my mind to see the whole picture. I was desperate to do it and to learn where I went wrong.

I could not believe that so much love that I felt was wasted and needed to be forgotten or switched off. There had to be other ways. And, as I have proven, they were not that difficult. All that was needed was time. I took the time to look at my perceptions of all the events of my life that seemed unfair or hurtful. I chose to find the other side, the side that was not seen at the time of the events. The side that is only able to be seen if we choose to take the time to look for it. The other side is always there.

My hope for the reader is that you will take the time to look for the other side of the events of your life. That when you get sad because someone acted a certain way, you choose to take time to see where the blessings are to that event. When you find those blessings, you become certain that there is no need to be upset, no need to forgive anything but only to say thank you to that person.

As Dr John Demartini said, "If we love people for who they are, they become the people we love". That sentence made sense to me straight away because I would always prefer to love, but it was not easy to love others as they are. Still, I persisted.

When I got upset, I would take time to see where I have done the same to others and what were the benefits to them. Then, I would find benefits to me because of what happened.

The benefits are always there if we are honest and patient enough to look. Once that is done, I would write a few words of thank you to the person who upset me. It was not for them to read, only for me to see how they have positively contributed to my life.

Those words of gratitude would come from my heart and were always honest. We cannot cheat ourselves into seeing something if we are not seeing it yet. That is why it takes time to clearly see the other side of every event.

Since I have been practicing loving others as they are, they started becoming the people I love. They would realise that I have dropped my judgment of their actions and love them as they are. When we are loved for who we are we try to be our best for those who grant us that love.

To love or not to love – that is the question. My answer is always to love. To love is a choice, just like staying angry at someone is a choice.

It seems easier to choose anger because we all like to be right and tell others how we want to be treated and loved. Choosing anger keeps us locked away from the gifts of love. Choosing love opens the gates for all the blessings we want.

Nuggets of Wisdom

I have shared some parts of my life with you to pass on the wisdom that I have gained on the way.

We all collect our nuggets of wisdom and try to apply them to enjoy a better quality of life. We are not here for a very long time. Half of that time we are trying to make sense of what is going on, and the second half we are hoping to get it right.

My mentor said, "It is better to have the wisdom of the ages without the aging process instead of the wisdom of the ages with the aging process."

Why have the wisdom of the ages with the aging process, when we can look in the moment and discover it, finding the wisdom of the ages without the aging process and see both sides that are there?

Some people will say that they are happy to make mistakes and learn their lessons. We do learn from our mistakes, and it is the best teacher, but I would rather be given the wisdom of the lessons learned and see if I can apply them instead of taking years to get my own answers.

We are born from love, and the biggest gift is to love and be loved. If we ask anyone who only has

24 hours to live, how would they want to spend that time? Almost everyone would say that they want to tell those around them that they loved them. Most of our regrets come from not letting go of hurts and from closing the heart to love.

My biggest wish for readers of my story is to let go of the hurts, blames, guilts and resentments. At any given time, we do our best, and others do as well. There is no point in going back and holding on to the thought that if we acted differently or someone else acted differently, then our lives would be better, would be different. This is because we have no certainty that it would be better.

I have learned that the only thing that gave me peace of mind and made sense in my life was when I found out that the so-called "problems" I had were all the outcomes of me choosing not to love.

Love is not that difficult. If we get worried about something or someone who has done something we don't like, it may not be easy to think about it with love straight away. Instead, we can try to redirect our thoughts to what is easier to love: nature, music, pets, people we love, activities we enjoy. It is about being in a state of as much love and appreciation as possible. It is about focusing our minds on the subjects that make us feel good.

What we focus on grows and when we focus on what brings us joy, it will bring more joyful experiences to our lives.

Letting go of what bothers us makes us free from focusing on what we don't like. In turn, we will not be attracting it back to our lives.

In this book I have included many exercises that I have used to turn my life around. I did them many times and continue to do so. We cannot change how we look at life and how we react if we don't use new ways of thinking. To be able to think differently, we need new ideas. It is not enough to read an affirmation or a sentence that makes sense and expect to gain the tools for new behaviour. We gained the knowledge then it needs to be applied.

To be able to apply it, the brain needs to learn new ways of processing those pieces of information. That is where retraining the brains comes into play.

It is like training to run a long distance. The runner trains every day, or at least a few times a week, and is focused on having a fit physical body.

To have a healthy mind – one that can cope with the strain of stressful situations – the mind needs to prepare itself to be trained and ready to take it on. I have achieved this by exercising it with the new ideas that I have learned.

There were many times when I was very upset, and taking time to find positives to the actions of someone who has hurt me was the last thing I wanted to do. But because I knew that it has worked wonders before, I was certain that if I got over my pride and did it, I would not only free my mind from the unnecessarily heavy burden, but also attract pleasant actions from others.

I became a coach and a teacher not to have a new profession but to share those tools with everyone who wants to learn it. I feel blessed to come across it, use it, master it and benefit from it in many ways. It gave me freedom from worries. It gave me peace. It brought me the freedom that I was searching for.

The decision of choosing to search for answers will gift you a life full of experiences that will not only broaden your horizons but will make your heart melt with joy, excitement and so much love that it will spill onto everyone around you. Light is the source of life. That light will be lit inside of you and make everything that you turn your attention to grow.

Keep asking questions, keep listening to your intuition, keep searching for wisdom that resonates with you and proves itself by giving you the life you want. Do not stop asking for improvement in all areas of your life. Like a tree that turns to the sun and searches for water, keep turning towards the light and thirst for the love that you deserve.

You were sent here to experience love and joy. Don't let anyone convince you that for some reason you are meant to suffer. No mother or father will wish for their child to suffer. No God or other deity that created us and put us on this earth want us to suffer. Not now, not in the afterlife.

Love feels light and good, and it is how we are meant to feel. No one ever says that they want less love. Hate and anger feel heavy and not good. No one wants to hold onto those emotions for long.

Make love your purpose in life. Choose love. Ask for love. Get to know love. In times of despair, loneliness and hurt, hold onto love. Find the form that represents love for you in times of need while you are waiting for the form that you want.

It may be a flower, a river, a song, a book, a pet, a memory or a friend. Anything and everything can represent love for you. Hold tightly onto it as if your life depended on it because it does.

Love is an inside job. It is a decision to choose to see it in what is around. It is the thought of wanting to feel connected to the love that created us. Love is what we are made of. Love can never be destroyed. I took the journey to discover that love embraces everything, it is created from the perfect balance of support and challenge. I looked for it outside of me while it was always there, in my own heart.

The willingness to love was there, the way I was going about it was not correct. I was expecting that if everything around me was well, then I would feel loved and love others. Instead, I was supposed to love first and keep loving no matter what, to be truly loved and know what love is. "There is only love, everything else is an illusion." Wise words from Dr John Demartini.

I found that love inside my own heart, and from there I chose to live, surrounded by the love from my beating heart. That is what I wish for you. Do not give up until you find yourself back in the comfort of your own heart, in the place that feels like you belong.

You have created the wish to be here, as you are, creating from love, creating love with every beat of your heart. Continue the journey. Keep it simple. Take one step at a time. Do not beat yourself up if things don't go as you wanted, it is only a detour. It may be taking you to the places that you have not planned, but nonetheless, those detours will be an experience that the universe has prepared for you so you can enjoy life to the full. They are necessary, and it is there where the magic of life will reveal itself to you.

Keep going. Keep noticing all the small stuff on the way. Be present with your mind and with your heart. Nature does not create in a hurry and it takes time to reveal its beauty.

Do not hurry through life. If you do, you may miss the most important parts, the ones that truly matter and will help you to open your heart to a better connection with yourself and with others. A lack of connections is the cause of addictions and heartache. To be able to connect from the heart, you need patience. Patience with yourself and patience with others.

Take as much time as you need to learn how to love others as they are. Keep searching for answers until you find them.

Part Summary – Key Points

1. Take the time to know what your current values are.

   Everything we experience is leading us toward what we truly value and want.

   Everyone is a "Messenger" of Love.

2. Fears are a part of life.

   The best way to overcome fears is to imagine them coming true and finding benefits to it.

   There is a strength in us that we are not aware of, and it is activated when needed.

3. Know what you want.

   We are here on this earth to experience joy through having desires and working to fulfil them.

   Imagination is the strongest force in a process of creation.

Conclusion

While here on this earth we are free to make choices. The biggest gift is that we can choose what we think. There were, are and will be things in our life that we cannot control and trying to do so creates unhappy life.

Controlling others or changing others is not possible; accepting them as they are is in our control. Choosing one thought over another is possible. It can be challenging sometimes, but with effort, it is achievable.

Wanting to have a happy life is a decision we all can make. Doing what it takes to achieve it is in our control. There is a reason why each of us are here, even if we do not understand it.

Accepting that we have a purpose, even when we feel lost, helps us to connect to everyone around us. We may look different, act differently, and think differently, but we all want the same things – to fit in, to be understood, to be accepted, to be appreciated, to be loved as we are.

If we look at ourselves with the eyes of our creator, we will see perfection. Nothing to add, nothing to take away. Nothing to change on the outside, nothing to change on the inside.

Like when we look at a flower, we do not say that it should look like a different flower. It is beautiful and perfect as it is, regardless of whether other flowers have different shapes and colours or smells.

Every flower is beautiful and perfect.

So is every person. Beautiful and perfect.

I have learned to not judge myself or compare myself to others. I have learned not to judge others. They are different, but perfect and beautiful, inside and out. I am different, but perfect and beautiful, inside and out.

*

The struggles that we must face in life are mostly not physical. We are spiritual beings having a physical experience. Most of the battles are fought in our minds. Questioning ourselves, questioning others. Comparing ourselves to others, judging others relative to our values. Feeling guilty, feeling hurt.

All these avalanches of thoughts will be our constant companion. I have learned to be kind to myself in my thoughts. I learned to see my thought as a phenomenon happening alongside me.

In the past, my thoughts and the heaviness of them have almost killed me. I wanted to control them, change them, but I did not know how. Since I learned to look at them as a part of me but not something that is all of me, it became easier to distance myself from them.

When heavy, fearful thoughts crowded my mind, I would recognise them as such. I would try to find where the fear is coming from. I would analyse them, break them down and find the other side to them – the hidden one.

So often we fear future losses just because we do not know how to change our thought. I started to pull my thoughts apart, break them down into small pieces, that I can understand better. When fear creeps in as a thought of a negative nature, I will keep asking myself what has caused it to appear and how much truth there is to it.

The best quote from Dr John Demartini is, "The quality of our lives is based on the quality of the questions we ask ourselves." After experiencing depression and hating the fact that I had a head full of thoughts that I could not switch off, I became someone whose favourite pastime is to think.

I love analysing what I am thinking now. I love choosing my thoughts. I love choosing thoughts that make me feel on top of the world and bring joy and excitement that could be compared to a physical orgasm. It became a fun experience.

I know that I do not need to control my thoughts, but I can redirect them if I choose to. It is said that thinking is the hardest thing to do, much harder than any physical work we may try to compare it to.

But it is the most rewarding. Mastering the art of thinking and being able to choose any thought at will is the most precious gift we can give to ourselves.

Achieving the ability
to choose our
thoughts and to
switch off the
unwanted ones frees
us from being a
slave to our minds
and makes us a
master of our
destiny.

THE SMALLEST STAR
I WILL TRY TO CATCH
AND QUICKLY WHISPER MY WISH.
I GRASP IN MY HANDS
THE WIND OF HOPE
PAINTED WITH THE COLOURS
OF THE NIGHT.

Acknowledgements

My Friend Irene, who first saw the writer in me.

Laura Hughes, for being my coach and trusted supporter.

My Ex-Husband, for being my companion for important part of my life, and for shaping up the woman in me. His actions and quest to find himself, has allowed me to look deeper into myself and discover the person I always wanted to be, and that *The Answer to Everything is Love.*

Emily Gowor, for acknowledging the gifts in me and helping me to bring them to the world.

Dr John Demartini, for teaching me what love is.

My Husband Gary, for showing me what unconditional love is through his words and actions. For being the supporter in all areas of my life and the challenger when I needed the push to grow. For his wisdom and big heart that saw the beauty and gifts in me that I sometimes struggle to see.

My children, for encouraging me to follow my souls calling and to share my gifts with the world. For their belief in me that I can be, do and have anything I am able to see in my future.

My Sisters, Ania and Dorka, for being the best siblings and friends I could asked for. The unshakable bond we share has made for an enjoyable, inspiring and meaningful journey.

My Dad, for putting me through the toughest lessons of my life, where I first learned fear and felt unloved. It is because of him I have been on the journey of learning unconditional love, the power of imagination and finding my purpose in life.

My Mama, for shaping me into the person who knows humility, patience, gratitude, courage, and the power of faith. She passed onto me the love of reading and learning. Her unconditional acceptance and appreciation of me as I was gave me the wings to fly higher that those around me and see the beauty in everything.

About The Author

Emilia Bruckner was born in Poland. She studied to be a librarian and was interested in literature and philosophies since she was a little girl. She worked for Polish government as an inspector, then emigrated to Italy when she was in her twenties. There she met her future husband, who she followed to Australia, his home country. After 15 years of marriage, having three children and establishing successful businesses, the relationship suddenly ended, and she spiralled into anxiety and depression. Unable to find help through established roads of counsellors and psychologists, she embarked on a journey to find answers to why she could not get herself out from the dark place in her mind.

She found and applied techniques that gave her not only relief from anxiety but answers to every *why* she always wanted answered.

Since then, she has remarried, become successful in all areas of life and made it her life's purpose to keep learning and discovering what life is about as well as coaching those who find themselves on similar journeys.

Her passion for sharing her love and wisdom become her driving force in life, and this book is the first one in a series of stories that become lessons of love, acceptance and appreciation.

For more information, visit
www.emiliabruckner.com.au

www.ingramcontent.com/pod-product-compliance
Ingram Content Group UK Ltd.
Pitfield, Milton Keynes, MK11 3LW, UK
UKHW062309290726
14090UKWH00018B/972